GARDENERS DIRECT LINES

Your questions answered by the BBC tv experts

GARDENERS DIRECT LINES

Your questions answered by the BBC tv experts

DAPHNE LEDWARD
PETER SEABROOK
GEOFFREY SMITH
BILL SOWERBUTTS
with JOHN THIRLWELL

BBC BOOKS

Published by BBC Books,
a division of BBC Enterprises Limited
Woodlands, 80 Wood Lane, London W12 0TT
First published 1988

ISBN 0 563 20693 4

Set in 10/11pt Baskerville, and printed in Great Britain
by Redwood Burn Limited, Trowbridge, Wiltshire

Cover printed by Fletchers of Norwich

CONTENTS
— ◆ —

ABOUT THE AUTHORS

DAPHNE LEDWARD was born in Bradford and now lives in Lincolnshire. Having worked as a landscape gardener for several years, she started the BBC Radio Lincolnshire *Gardening Programme* and became a frequent contributor to Radio 4's *Gardeners' Question Time*. She now divides her time between broadcasting, writing, lecturing and garden design consultancy.

PETER SEABROOK received a national diploma from the Royal Horticultural Society and has over 30 years' experience in horticultural production and retailing. A working director of two national garden centre companies, he has also become an author of gardening books, gardening correspondent on several newspapers and magazines, and presenter of a number of programmes on American and British television, including *Gardeners' World* and *The Chelsea Flower Show* for the BBC.

GEOFFREY SMITH studied at the Askham Bryan Horticultural College. For 20 years he was the Superintendent of the Northern Horticultural Society's Garden at Harlow Car, Harrogate, and he now works as a freelance writer and broadcaster. He is the author of many best-selling books on garden cultivation and has presented a number of popular gardening programmes on BBC television, including *Mr Smith's Gardening Series* and *Geoffrey Smith's World of Flowers*. He was a regular panel member on *Gardeners' Question Time* for 11 years.

BILL SOWERBUTTS lives in Lancashire and has been a gardening correspondent on national and local newspapers for more than 35 years. He was one of the original contributors to *Gardeners' Question Time* (recording over 1500 programmes) and has appeared on numerous television programmes about gardening.

INTRODUCTION
♦

FAR AND AWAY THE MOST COMMON QUESTION
people ask about *Gardeners' Direct Line* is: 'If it's a live
show, how come the gardeners always manage to have the
right plants there to answer the questions?'

Now I'm going to sort the matter out once and for all.
Briefly, it works like this: we open the phone lines in the
morning so that by lunchtime we can choose the problems
we're going to answer and get the plants and props into
the studio in time for transmission. Then when we go on
the air we actually *call back* the people who'd rung in
before.

Geoffrey is the regular expert on the show, while Peter
tends to alternate with either Bill Sowerbutts, Stefan Buz-
cacki or Daphne Ledward. At 10.30 the gardeners and I
go into the studio and record the 'trails' – those 30-second
clips trailing the programme and the phone number. Two
trails guarantee us several thousand calls, although the
show's number is now so well known that the lines are
busy the moment they open.

As the calls come in they are logged and passed on to
our gardening adviser, Daphne Ledward. Over the next
two hours she consults with the other gardeners, and
together they pick out the best 15 questions. While all this
is going on, we are calling the Leeds garden centre which
supplies most of the 'props'. The manager, Bert Carling,
and his team start to load up their trailer; as a question is
picked for the show, the necessary plant is chosen. If we
need a plant that is diseased or in any way blighted, we'll
probably go to the Leeds Parks department for help;
there, Joe Maiden is invariably able to lay his hands on
just the right example. As you can imagine, getting hold of
plants that have 'gone wrong' is more difficult than find-
ing perfect specimens.

By two o'clock Daphne and the team will have decided upon the final list of questions. They choose as wide a variety as possible, and with an eye to the weather and season. They also try to 'spread' the calls around the country, but if two good calls happen to come in from the same town then they'll both be included. It's more important that we cover all the most common problems than do justice to every part of the British Isles!

Between 2.00 and 3.00 p.m. the studio will be 'stocked' with all the necessary props. Meanwhile, the producer's assistant rings the 15 callers whose questions have been chosen to make sure they'll be in when the show goes on air. (There have been times when we've rung back to find them out.) In the studio, the gardeners and I make sure we know where the necessary plants are for each question.

Twenty-five minutes from transmission we have a technical rehearsal. *Gardeners' Direct Line* is a remarkably complicated show to broadcast, and it is to the great credit of the BBC engineers at Leeds that we have never yet got into serious difficulties while on the air.

The rehearsal finishes about five minutes from transmission, which gives the producer time to come down from the control room to give us all last minute words of advice. The show is entirely unscripted and at this stage the only likely directions are going to be about particular camera shots for the gardeners to be aware of as they do their demonstrations.

One minute to go and the production assistant begins her count-down to the start of the programme. In the studio, Geoff and Peter are straining at the leash to get going.

'And now on BBC 1, John Thirlwell and the team bring you *Gardeners' Direct Line*.'

Our titles begin. We're on the air and it's time to start answering a few questions. And that brings me to this book.

After several series of *Gardeners' Direct Line*, it dawned upon us that perhaps we could help struggling gardeners everywhere by putting the most common problems into a book for all to read at their leisure. You'll see that we have divided the problems into five main categories, and each has its own chapter. I shall introduce each one, just as I would do on the programme, but having said my piece I shall shut up and let the experts do the clever stuff.

JOHN THIRLWELL

LAWNS

THERE'S NOTHING LIKE A GOOD LAWN TO MAKE your garden look superb. Immaculately cut, it spreads like an expensive green carpet across your chosen acre, setting off the rest of the shrubs and plants a treat. The only trouble is that good lawns are remarkably difficult to maintain, especially if you have a young family. Bicycles, football boots and (albeit during the summer months only) paddling pools are the arsenal of the young. And, of course, if the family has a dog – particularly if it's a female – then your lawn will be subjected to indescribable abuse. I know this from personal experience.

Once, when answering a lawn question, Geoffrey almost took the programme off the air. He was about to demonstrate a small electric mower and placed it on a tiny patch of turf that was the studio lawn.

'They're not bad little things these really,' he said. 'And all you've got to do is pull this lever here . . .'

The mower – which everybody had assumed was unplugged – roared into life. Chaos ensued. Apart from deafening us all, the mower jammed all the radio mikes and the 'talkback' intercom between the studio and the control room. One of the big 'key' lights began to flicker. A cameraman woke up. The show was about to go rapidly off the air when Geoff let go of the lever, and the mower stopped. We heaved a mighty sigh and continued. From that day, every electrical 'prop' is double-checked before we go on air!

Anyway, enough of the BBC's problems, what about yours?

JOHN THIRLWELL

Two years ago I had field drains laid under my lawn and although this has cured the drainage problem I am now left with uneven areas where the trenches were dug. The grass generally is in good condition, so is it possible to level the lawn without digging it up and starting again?

PETER   Fortunately, yes. Hollows of all kinds are quite easily levelled by slowly adding thin layers of good new soil. Gardeners in years gone by used old potting compost for this. Today in the age of soil-less potting composts, it is better to use either a compost mix of good garden soil (7 parts by volume), moss peat (3 parts by volume) and coarse sand (2 parts by volume). Or, if you haven't got all these materials, good garden soil will do for hollow filling.

This job is best done in spring or autumn when the soil is damp and the grass is growing strongly. Spread up to 1 inch (2.5 cm) deep over the grass in the hollow and lightly rake it into the turf. After three weeks or so the grass will grow up through the new soil. Once really well through and re-established, just add another layer of soil or compost. Keep doing this until the surface is level.

If you put down too thick a layer at one go and suffocate the grass beneath, just re-seed with more lawn seed. The trick here is to distribute the new seed mixture over the bare patch and into the surrounding turf rather like darning a hole in a sock. Then new and old grass intermix and the patch doesn't grow a different shade of green.

Humps are much more difficult to level. Here a 1 inch (2.5 cm) deep 'H' shape cut is made across the hump and two or more turves are cut and rolled back from the cross cut (see illustration). Soil is then shovelled from the opened up area before replacing the turves in the lower position. I find it quite difficult to get the turves back level; they usually sink too much and it is then necessary to add some soil to level the new hollow!

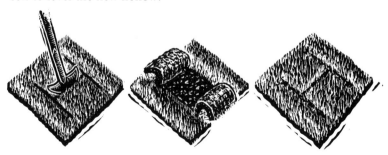

Levelling a hump

My soil is heavy, wet clay and I am about to put down a new lawn. Could you advise me on how to go about preparing the ground, and in your opinion, will I get a good lawn from seed or would turf be a better proposition?

GEOFFREY A heavy clay soil offers no handicap to the work of producing a good lawn providing care is taken to ensure it is free draining, except, of course, the work of preparation will be considerably harder. There are compensations, for I have more problems with my present lawn laid down on sandy soil than with the acre and more in my last garden where the terrain was glacial clay.

To make sure surplus water drains away quickly, work the soil to a depth of at least 15 inches (38 cm). Deep digging, working in well rotted organic matter at the same time, breaks up the sub-soil to let excess rain water drain through, and improves the soil structure. During the digging remove any perennial weeds, especially couch grass which is impossible to get rid of once the lawn is established. Where possible, particularly with a clay soil, do the heavy digging in autumn so that the alternate wet/dry, freeze/thaw of winter can work on the intractable clods to leave a workable tilth in early May. Before working the soil down for turfing or sowing, I put on a dressing of fertiliser containing a high proportion of superphosphate to ensure healthy root growth.

Grow your lawn from seed obtained from a reputable source. That way you can choose a grass mixture to suit precisely the soil and your purpose. The lawn may take a month or two longer in establishing but it will be considerably less expensive than buying turf. You will also have a better control of quality than is possible when buying turf.

Should you decide to lay turf instead of sowing seed, inspect the quality before placing an order. Make sure the sward is largely composed of fine-leaved grasses. Reject any turf containing couch or soft-grass or too many perennial weeds, particularly creeping buttercup.

Whether sowing seed or laying turf, do make certain that the area which is to be transformed into a lawn is perfectly level. Leave no hills to be scalped bare with the mower, or hollows to fill with water.

Deep digging (or double digging)

I have recently bought a bitch puppy, and where she has 'spent a penny' on the lawn the grass has died in some places and turned dark green and coarse in others. Is there anything I can treat it with to restore it?

DAPHNE   It is the urea in the dog's urine, a rich source of fast-acting nitrogen, which is the problem. It's rather like overdosing the grass with a high-nitrogen fertiliser. Usually it is only a superficial burning that causes the brown patches and eventually the roots will regrow, but unfortunately on a high quality turf some of the finer grasses can be killed out altogether. The dark green colour is due to a boost in growth by the nitrogen and will eventually fade. The patches may be coarser because the finer grasses have disappeared.

There really isn't anything you can do to prevent this kind of lawn damage other than keeping the dog off altogether or watching her every movement and dashing out with a watering can to dilute the urine patch immediately. From my own experience, I find that the best solution is to train the puppy to use one part of the garden as a 'loo' – preferably gravelled so it can be regularly watered with a disinfectant. Dogs and high quality lawns really don't go together very well and it is as well to recognise this fact before acquiring a pup if you are very lawn-proud.

If you haven't fed your lawn regularly and it is looking yellow, the 'bitch spots' can look even worse, so a quick cosmetic job can be effected by watering the whole lawn with a half-strength solution of a liquid 'green-up' lawn fertiliser twice, allowing a fortnight between applications. This should make the grass greener and so the spots less obvious. Dead patches which don't regrow can be scratched over and reseeded in the autumn or spring.

Could you give me some tips on caring for a recently seeded lawn? For example, when should it have its first cut, and can I use weedkillers to kill the weed seedlings which seem almost as numerous as the grass?

BILL   The best times to sow lawn grass seed are either the first week in September or the first week in April, though local weather and soil conditions do dictate the timing of such a sowing.

Very important also is the previous preparation of the area to be sown. It should be turned over either with a spade or fork, or maybe with a powered rotary cultivator, ideally to a depth of around 8 inches (20 cm).

You can control weed seedlings prior to sowing by creating a seed bed to stimulate germination, spraying off the seedlings with Weedol and repeating if there is a high population of weed seeds in the soil. It is important to clear weeds before sowing as there is not a suitable weedkiller available for new lawns.

If the drainage is suspect then ideally rubble or tile drains should be installed. Poor drainage, of course, will soon become evident when water stands on the area for more than 24 hours.

Next comes the choice of seed to be sown. The modern dwarf rye-grass seed mixtures are very good for lawns which are going to be subject to heavy use. (See also pages 14–15.) If you want a much finer grass for purely ornamental purposes, then sow a completely rye-free mixture.

The obvious advantage of having dwarf-growing grasses is that they need less frequent mowing.

The first mowing should be done when the seedling grasses are about 2^1/$_2$ inches (6 cm) high. You should use a cylinder mower without the grass box and with the blade set quite high. It must be a mower with sharp blades or it will tend to snatch the seedlings out of the soil. With very small areas, it probably pays to use sharp shears for this first clipping.

Many weed seedlings will be present, but many of these will vanish under later, closer mowing. Persistent weeds that won't mow out, such as daisies, plantains, pearl-wort, clover and speedwell, will need to be treated later with a selective hormone weedkiller between April and September, when the grass is well established. Check the product label for the timing of application to newly-sown lawns.

I have just acquired an established high quality lawn and I want to keep it that way. Can you give me some tips for summer maintenance and the best autumn treatment to ensure it survives the winter?

DAPHNE   No lawn will stay in first-class condition unless it is fed to replace what is removed week after week as cuttings. A high nitrogen fertiliser – which boosts growth and improves colour – should be given once the grass is in active growth, usually from early May. However, it should not be applied after the middle of August as it will produce lush grass prone to winter diseases. An autumn lawn food, which you apply in September or October, contains very little nitrogen but is high in potash and phosphates, which toughen up the grass.

Summer lawn foods are of two types; those which are applied dry, preferably with a spreader for even dispersal, and those which are watered on. The latter are useful for an instant 'green-up' and are easily put on without overdosing, but they need regular application because the effect soon wears off. Dry fertilisers only have to be used once or twice a season, especially the modern ones which contain nitrogen in a slow-release form. They must be applied evenly though, or browning and patchy colour will occur.

As yours is a fine lawn, weeds should not be a problem, but odd ones can be dealt with by using a liquid or solid wax-based product available for spot treatment of lawn weeds.

A lawn should never be mown too short, although fine lawns can be cut shorter than coarse ones. A scalped lawn will be open to all sorts of problems – weed invasion, moss, drought damage and the like. It is better to cut slightly longer and more often. Early or late cuts should always be made with the blades set high, gradually lowering them as the season progresses, but raising them again in hot, dry weather. The clippings should be removed, except during drought, when they can be left on to give protection. If you have to water, give a good soaking – dribbles can do more harm than good.

In September the lawn can be raked lightly with a mechanical or spring-tined rake to remove dead material, but thorough scarifying should be left until spring or frost damage may occur. Spiking compacted ground with a spiker or hollow-tined fork will let in the air and improve the health of the grass. I like to top-dress the lawn after spiking using a mixture similar to Peter's recommendation for filling hollows (see page 3), or a proprietory lawn dressing, applied at 3 lb per sq yd and brushed in so the grass isn't smothered.

Fallen leaves should be removed immediately, using a soft leaf rake or a soft brush. A metal rake will eventually remove all the grass too!

◇

I'm thinking of offering my lawn to a natural history museum as it's a botanical paradise, with speedwell, docks, daisies, dande-lions, clover, buttercups, yarrow and a lot of other weeds I can't identify. How can I eradicate them?

PETER Most of the weeds you list, and many others not listed, are easily controlled by the correct application of selective lawn weed-killers. This is the sequence to follow for the quickest and most complete result.

If the grass is poor as well as very weedy, you should start with a fertiliser application and thorough raking in spring or autumn. Then when the grass in the lawn is growing strongly, late April to September, mow it. Leave for at least three days or so for young weed leaves to unfold, then water the turf with diluted selective lawn weedkiller to the manufacturer's instruction.

A watering can and fine rose delivers small water droplets and provides a good weed-leaf cover. Apply the weedkiller when the weather is calm to prevent drift in the wind onto adjacent garden plants. The weather is usually still in the early morning and late evening. Always wash the can out thoroughly after use and ideally keep a separate red watering can for weedkillers.

Once lawn weedkillers have dried on the leaves they will be safe to pets and animals. Leave the lawn for as long as possible before mowing again; this allows the weedkiller to travel right down in the sap to the weed roots, which usually takes five days in warm weather.

Very deep rooted, big patches of weeds and certain resistant weeds such as speedwell may need another treatment in a month or two; alternatively, they can be spot-treated with a convenient trig-ger-spray product. Once the weeds are under control, the appli-cation of a combined weed-and-feed each spring is usually all it takes to keep the lawn weed-free.

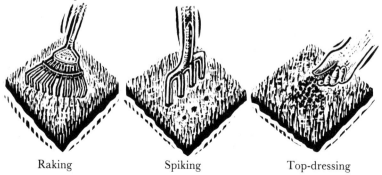

Raking   Spiking   Top-dressing

Where you have specific weeds such as clover or speedwell, check the different brands of lawn weedkillers and select one which lists the kinds you want to control. Water-based weedkillers tend to run off upright, spiky weeds, like yarrow, and treating these with a wax-based weedkiller stick, that adheres to the leaves, will be more effective.

Over the last two years I have noticed an increasing amount of moss in my lawn, and where it is shaded there is also liverwort and black slimy patches. The soil is heavy clay. Is there a satisfactory remedy?

GEOFFREY Getting rid of moss from a lawn presents no real problem; with modern methods of control it really is quite easy. The hard part is stopping it coming back.

On a clay soil, poor drainage combined with surface compaction leaves roots starved of air and, curious as it may seem, moisture. Spiking, using deep slitting blades or a hollow-tine fork, will alleviate both conditions. After treating the turf, brush coarse sand into the surface to fill the air channels and keep them open.

Starvation is another contributory factor, for the grass then fails to form a thick enough sward to prevent moss spores gaining access. Regular feeding will relieve this particular state of affairs.

Check that the soil acidity is not too low, which can weaken grass and encourage moss. It can easily be balanced with a top dressing of lime, taking care not to lift the pH above neutral.

Finally, set the blades of the mower so that they do not shave the grass. Never cut the grass closer than ³/₄ to 1 inch (2 to 2.5 cm) unless, of course, you are preparing a bowling green finish.

Having decided on the possible causes, before putting them right just get rid of the moss by applying a proprietory mosskiller. Any one of the several available will do the job: you could try one of the products containing dichlorophen alone or in a mixture with ferrous sulphate and chloroxuron. With the latter, longer term control can be achieved, so that the treatment does not need to be repeated more than once a year. The traditional lawn sand offers a reasonably cheap alternative and can be made up as follows: 10 parts by weight lime-free sand, 3 parts by weight sulphate of ammonia, 1 or 2 parts by weight calcined sulphate of iron (ferrous sulphate). Apply the mixture evenly over the lawn surface at the rate of 4 oz per sq yd (140 gm per sq m) when the soil is moist. The moss will turn black and, if all goes well, die and can then be raked out and disposed of.

Trees causing over-dense shade may need pruning back to let in more light. Liverwort and the black slimy algae will be destroyed by the mosskiller. Routine spiking, feeding and, under certain conditions, top-dressing with sterilised soil will complete the process.

Where the shade is particularly dense, digging the decrepit lawn up and then re-seeding with a shade-tolerant grass mixture may be the best long-term solution.

Help, please! There are more molehills than grass on my lawn. Can these pests be exterminated? I'm told it's impossible.

DAPHNE   I'm rather inclined to agree! Moles are attracted by worms and slugs, so if you have a lot of these, especially if your garden is large with plenty of undisturbed areas, and borders on farmland, you are quite likely to encounter them at some time.

Moles tunnel the ground looking for suitable food. As the enormous amount of soil moved while doing this has to go somewhere, it is periodically forced up to the surface where it creates the dreaded molehill. Once the mole has found an adequate supply of worms, it stops tunnelling and creates a 'larder', storing surplus worms by biting off their heads.

Poor soils with a low worm population are less interesting to moles, and, as they are shy animals, small, well-used gardens are often given a miss because they don't like all the above-ground activity.

Getting rid of these pests is easier said than done. Obviously cutting down the food supply helps, so leaves should always be raked up off the grass in autumn to avoid increasing the worm population. Proprietory lawn pestkillers can be applied but these are becoming more and more unpopular with the environmental sector of the gardening fraternity. Mole smokes are available; these are lit and placed down the runs, and recently there has appeared an ultrasonic device which is inserted into the run with the body of the appliance above ground. This is supposed to emit vibrations which the moles do not like. They probably will desert the run – only to appear a few feet away. Poking strong-smelling things down the runs, which is often recommended, will have the same effect. Mole traps, properly set, are still about the most efficient method of killing them, but it's a skilled job, so it's wise to get a knowledgeable mole-catcher to show you how, or do the job for you. Poisoned baits are not available to the amateur – they can only be used by a professional pest exterminator (see the *Yellow Pages* for your local officer). The best mole deterrent I know is our cat – apart from disturbing the ground above the tunnels he will actually catch and kill the little vandals.

I've got a lot of brown patches on my lawn and I don't have a dog. The problem is worst in autumn, though I do have some dead areas in spring as well.

BILL   There are a few possible reasons for these brown patches on your lawn. You do say that that the problem is worst in autumn, and this would suggest that the problem may be due to that bumbling wanderer the daddy-long-legs. This lays eggs in turf in autumn, leatherjackets are produced, and these gnaw away at the grass roots, causing brown, usually fairly circular patches. Cutworms underground can also lead to similar troubles.

The control is to use carbaryl or chlordane, strictly according to directions. These chemicals will kill any soil pests in the turf and will also reduce the number of earthworms, which in turn will mean that you probably don't have any trouble from moles.

Another possible explanation for these patches is that they follow the grass disease fusarium which is usually first seen towards the end of autumn and persists throughout the winter. The grasses may grow away satisfactorily the following spring, after aeration. The control for this disease is aeration and drenching with benomyl fungicide. The proper use of a lawn fertiliser also helps reduce the effects of the disease.

A less likely cause is poor drainage in that particular area. Hollow-tine spiking and re-seeding in spring would solve the problem.

What causes fairy rings and can I treat them?

GEOFFREY Certainly nothing so romantic as little people cavorting around in the moonlight. Toadstools may seem mundane by comparison, yet the ring effect is created simply by a fungus growth underground spreading out wider and wider. Several different species of toadstool can cause rings and with some, if not all, control is extremely difficult.

Where this disease produces lush dark green rings, there are various chemicals available that are reputed to give a complete control by liquid application once the area has been thoroughly spiked using a fork. However, I confess to taking an easy way out by just feeding the infected areas with extra nitrogen in the form of lawn sand. First, however, spike the discoloured turf, allowing a considerable overlap so that none of the infected soil is missed. The reason for this is that the underground fungal growth effectively waterproofs the soil. Spiking completed, apply the lawn sand and water it well in.

For those fungi producing a ring of dead grass, a more thorough approach is needed. Unfortunately, there is no suitable chemical to water onto the infected area.

One control, laborious beyond belief, is to remove the soil and turf to a depth of 10 to 12 inches (25 to 30 cm) over the whole area, and at least 14 inches (36 cm) at either side of the ring line. Taking care not to spill a crumb, carry all the soil away, then fill the hole with sterilised loam and re-turf. Before taking on such a Herculean labour, try the simple spike-and-feed approach. Even if the fungus is not completely killed, the reinvigorated rich green growth of grass completely masks out the tell-tale rings.

Alternatively, remove the turf plus as much root as possible and then sterilise the soil beneath with a product containing tar acid (tar oil). Leave the treated soil for approximately eight weeks and then seed or re-turf.

I have patches of coarse grass in my otherwise fine lawn. Can these be treated?

BILL It would have helped me if I had known whether your lawn was grown from seed or whether it was produced by laying turves. Very frequently lawn turf is sold that has patches of coarse grasses such as Yorkshire fog, Timothy, and some of the coarser strains of rye-grass. It is a fact that under ideal conditions of management these coarse grasses can eventually be mown out. The treatment consists of hollow-tine forking of the turf in March and again in early September. In late March or so, depending on the nature of the turf, if it is sticky and slow draining, then brush coarse sand into the spike holes, plus sulphate of ammonia mixed with the sand at the rate of no more than 1 oz per sq yd (35 gm per sq m). If on the other hand the lawn is on sand or shale and dries out very quickly, then brush fine moss peat into the spike holes, plus again sulphate of ammonia at 1 oz per sq yd (35 gm per sq m).

Following the spiking in autumn, what you brush into the core holes again depends on the nature of the soil – sticky heavy soil, brush sand into the spike holes; quick-draining soil, brush moss peat into the spike holes plus autumn turf fertiliser at 2 oz per sq yd (70 gm per sq m).

Another old technique of controlling coarse grasses, and indeed any coarse-bladed weeds, is in spring to use lawn sand which contains sulphate of iron and sulphate of ammonia. If this is not very effective, try killing off patches with Weedol or Tumbleweed, or digging out the weed grass and re-seeding or turfing.

Lawn sand works on a very simple principle of actually settling on the broad-leaved grasses or weeds and scorching and burning them to destruction. On the other hand, it falls away from the finer leaved, desirable grasses and far from damaging them it actually stimulates them into growth. And so eventually the nature of the grasses on the lawn changes from the coarse to the fine.

I am about to seed a new lawn and I have three children under six years old. What is the best mix to use?

PETER You are quite right to use the word mix. Nearly all lawn seed is a mixture of different kinds. Where the lawn will be used a lot by young children – and older people playing sports and causing much wear and tear – then a mixture containing some rye-grass should be chosen.

In the past, all rye-grasses had very deep, strong roots, and were tall, leafy and strong-growing, recovering quickly from wear and tear but also needing a lot of cutting. Modern varieties of rye-grass, however, combine deep, strong roots with much smaller, fine leaves and good winter colour, and needing less frequent cutting.

Look for names on the pack such as 'Elka', 'Hunter', 'Manhatten', 'Sprinter', 'Troubador' and 'Bellatrix', all fine leaved rye-grasses. The last two are especially fine-leaved. I have seen lawns of fine rye-grass fit to start using in two months from sowing in warm, damp weather. Also seed, including 'Hunter', sown as late as November in Essex, produced a green lawn by the following April.

A seed rate of 1 lb (450 gm) to 10 sq yd (10 sq m) will give a quick and dense cover. Do not rake the soil down too fine before sowing. If there are walnut-sized lumps at this stage they will break up after subsequent rain. Very fine soil, especially heavy clays, will run together after heavy rain and then dry into a hard skin, checking seed growth.

You will get a more even spread of seed by standing upright and scattering from waist height. In my view, Peter Russell (gardening correspondent on *House and Garden*) has the best method; he measures out 1¹/₂ oz (40 gm), spreads this evenly over 1 sq yd (1 sq m) and uses this as a visual guide for the thickness to apply over the rest of the area.

Regular overseeding of any badly worn patches in the future with a similar grass seed mixture, just as they do at Wimbledon and on the Wembley pitch, will quickly repair damage.

ORNAMENTALS
◆

WHEN THE BBC ORIGINALLY ASKED ME TO PRESENT
Gardeners' Direct Line, I thought they must have gone mad.

'But I don't know the first thing about gardening!'

'Exactly,' they replied.

Heigh ho, I thought, I'll give it a try. When the first series is over they'll see their mistake, axe the programme, and we can all go our separate ways. Umpteen series later, I'm beginning to see why they chose an ignoramus to front the show. The fact is that gardening *frightens* a lot of people, and if a viewer feels there's at least one other person around whose horticultural knowledge is minimal, then so much the better.

Now you may be wondering what all this has to do with 'ornamentals'. I still know very little about gardening but a little research tells me that a rose is an ornamental, as are numerous shrubs. Someone once told me that roses existed long before mankind ever appeared on this planet. It must have been a lovely place then. Actually, looking at the various flower-beds in my garden you could be forgiven for thinking that the primeval jungle must have looked positively sparse in comparison . . . I'd better read this chapter carefully!

JOHN THIRLWELL

Last year my roses suffered badly from greenfly, mildew and black spot and I even noticed what I thought was rust. I sprayed them but it had no effect. Is there a really effective treatment? Also, can I do anything else, like feeding, to ensure the bushes are strong enough to resist such problems?

DAPHNE   A good broad spectrum insecticide, used according to the manufactuer's instructions, will kill greenfly (aphids) but the problem can return, especially following inefficient spray application which leaves survivors which multiply rapidly, or when there is a continuous invasion of aphids from near by. There is no chemical which will last a whole season – even systemic insecticides, which work by entering the plant tissue and killing pests as they feed, only last a certain time. Left uncontrolled, greenfly distort leaves and flowerbuds, and their sticky secretions encourage the unsightly sooty mould disease to develop. The best solution is to spray at the first signs of infestation with an insecticide of low toxicity to higher animals, such as pirimicarb, pyrethrum or permethrin, which kills aphids but does not affect beneficial insects like bees, ladybirds and lacewings.

Mildew, black spot and rust are fungal diseases and have become much more common since the Clean Air Act prevented large emissions of sulphur-laden smoke from domestic fires and factories. Black spot is worse in warm, wet summers and starts as black spots with yellow edges on the leaves which then spread rapidly until the leaves fall off. Apart from being unsightly, the defoliation it causes weakens the bushes.

Mildew often starts late in the season as a result of dry roots, insufficient air movement around the bushes, hot days and cool nights. It appears as a white powdery substance which distorts young leaves and buds.

Rust is encouraged by cold springs and severe winters. It shows as orange pustules turning black on the undersides of the leaves. All diseases are made worse by shortage of potash and lack of food in general, so two applications of a high-potash specific rose food, one after pruning, the other after the first flush of flowers, helps to build up the plants.

It is much easier to prevent diseases than to cure them. Preventative spraying with any approved fungicide – benomyl, thiophanate-methyl, propiconazole, bupirimate, triforine, etc. – starting when the leaves unfurl and continuing at monthly intervals throughout the summer, is the best remedy. Some products are a combination of insecticide and fungicide, and sometimes a foliar feed as well. Changing the chemical periodically avoids building up a resistance to it by the pests and diseases. Clearing up all diseased matter as soon as possible, burning it or burying it deep, stops the spread of infection.

How should I prune neglected rose bushes? What is the correct time and how far back should they be pruned?

BILL   First we must presume that you are asking about neglected bush roses. Shrub or species roses are frequently described as bush roses, but most of these are very vigorous and really need little or no pruning except to remove entirely some of the central canes so that air movement is free and light is available.

It pays to half-prune bush roses in mid- to late November, even though some of them may still have some rather tired flowers on them. This half-pruning is intended to induce dormancy and reduce or eliminate wind-rock.

Another important point is that it pays with all roses to spray them with tar acid wash when they are fully dormant in late December. It obviously makes sense to spray the smaller, pruned rose rather than to spray the whole bush before pruning. The soil underneath the rose bush should also be sprayed with tar acid wash, providing there are no green plants there or bulbs just nosing through.

Around late March you then carry out the final lower pruning. Generally it pays to prune all bush roses very hard back around that time to 6 inches (15 cm) or so of soil level. The pruning cut should be

Hard pruning; showing
correct sloping cut

a   Not close enough to bud
b   Not clean enough
c   Not far enough from bud

just above an obvious growth eye, and ideally one pointing outwards so that you produce a goblet-shaped bush.

Very vigorous varieties, such as 'Queen Elizabeth', if not hard pruned, can get up to 6 feet (180 cm) or so, but if you prune them very hard they will flower at about 3½ feet (107 cm).

This hard-pruning of roses, and indeed of many other flowering shrubby subjects, is known as rejuvenation by reduction. It will work with a shrub, a hedge or with a rose, particularly a neglected one. What you are doing is giving the undisturbed root system less work to do, and it responds by producing vigorous top growth.

Composting the root spread, plus a few handfuls of Growmore fertiliser, completes the 'cure'.

I have an Acer pseudoplatanus 'Brilliantissimum' and every spring the leaves turn brown just before opening. How can I prevent this?

GEOFFREY 'Brilliantissimum' is a slow-growing form of the common sycamore whose leaves in spring open a delicate shade of shrimp pink. Unfortunately, the beauty is short lived and in maturity the foliage is liable to become disfigured by the black patches caused by the 'tar spot' fungus which is common and widespread on all sycamores.

The black blotches surrounded by a ring of yellow form on the upper surface of the leaves. Fortunately, the disease has no obvious harmful effect on the vigour and general well being of the tree. Gathering up the infected leaves as they fall and spraying with a Bordeaux mixture in late May and again in mid-summer may help reduce infection. Then bury them or take them to the local rubbish tip.

Is there any way of pruning a 12-year old, 20 feet (6 m) high weeping willow tree to keep it a manageable size? My neighbour is worried the roots could damage his drains.

DAPHNE   Your neighbour could be right. Apart from the nuisance the leaves cause and the amount of light blocked by a large weeping willow sited too near a property, on heavy soils the moisture removed by a weeping willow in full leaf can cause subsidence and eventual structural damage. Thirsty roots in search of moisture can penetrate and block drains and sewers. The removal of a problem tree can also give trouble when large quantities of moisture cease to be extracted from the soil; swelling and 'heave' can occur and cause structural damage.

Pretty as it is when young, the modern garden is no place for the golden weeping willow, *Salix chrysocoma* (*S. alba* 'Tristis'), or any other large tree for that matter. It can be lopped, but even though the resulting mass of young branches is pretty in summer, the winter silhouette of a lopped weeping willow is grotesque. Furthermore, once a large weeping willow is lopped, it will have to be done regularly, at least every two years, or it will quickly be back to its original height.

If you really want a weeping willow, try *Salix caprea* 'Pendula', the weeping Kilmarnock willow. This is an altogether better proposition for most gardens and is covered in fluffy grey 'pussy' catkins in early spring as a bonus. However, in form it is perhaps not as attractive as the American weeping willow, *Salix purpurea* 'Pendula' which has long, thin, heavily weeping branches, purple-tinged and covered in slender blue-green leaves.

Certain shrubs in our garden refuse to flower. The worst offenders are Kolkwitzia amabilis and Magnolia soulangeana. What can we feed them with to encourage flowering?

PETER   The successful treatment could well be different for each shrub. First the *Kolkwitzia amabilis* is best grown in a sunny position. In rich soil and shade, they may grow strongly but flower little. Some kolkwitzia sold are inferior seedlings and here again they may grow too well at the expense of flowering.

When either buying these plants, or digging suckers to form new plants, or rooting cuttings in summer, always seek out a good cultivar such as *K. a.* 'Pink Cloud', which was raised in the Royal Horticultural Society's Gardens, Wisley, Surrey. If you have done this and the only position you have is shaded, then some sulphate of potash in spring may help toughen the growth and encourage flowering.

If the magnolia you have is currently labelled *Magnolia* x *soulangeana* then you have a good flowering kind. Non-flowering is usually the result of the nurseyman's method of cultivation. When they are container-grown, i.e. pot-grown, plants suffer no root check when transplated into our gardens. Quite a lot of this species of magnolia and several others, however, are grown in Holland in open fields of black, peaty soil. While they grow well in this, when lifted with a ball of soil which is held in place with sacking, there is quite a lot of root damage. Add to this the period out of the ground and in transit and you will appreciate the plant has a severe check.

Even loosely potted before sale, this type of 'balled plant' will take several years to recover, especially if planted in heavy clay soil or light sandy soil. The test of a good container-grown plant is one which can be carefully lifted by the stem without the pot and some soil falling off. If there are a *few* new roots coming out of the base of the pot, showing root activity, and developing flower buds above, that is even better.

Once again, if the plant has not suffered this kind of check and is growing well but not flowering, apply some potash fertiliser in spring or early summer.

We are shortly moving house and hope, with the new owner's permission, to take several fairly large shrubs with us. How do we go about preparing them so they transplant successfully?

PETER   Most deciduous shrubs, which lose their leaves each autumn, can be moved from mid-October to early March. Evergreens, on the other hand, are best transplanted September/October or March/April. Moved at this time, new roots are quickly made to help sustain the evergreen foliage. Even so, plants like holly (*Ilex*) may drop their leaves and then grow new ones.

Some plants do not respond well to digging up and transplanting, for example brooms (*Cytisus*), firethorns (*Pyracantha*), clematis, ceanothus and vines (*Vitis*). If the plants will transplant but you are moving at the wrong time of year, they are best lifted at the right time and grown for several months in some good potting compost either in large pots or in thick polythene bags with drainage holes. Lifted plants can then be put in a shady place and kept well watered while they make new roots and start to recover from the root damage.

Fairly large shrubs and young trees will move best if the large outer roots can be cut six months or so before moving. Draw a circle 1 to 2 feet (30 to 60 cm) out from the stem or trunk and dig a trench to one spade's depth around the outer edge. Keep the inner soil well watered and new fibrous roots will form within the circle. If you can get help to lift or move a larger circle of soil and root, so much the better, but a ball 2 to 3 feet (60 to 90 cm) across is as heavy as most people can manage.

When you are ready to move the plants, cut the soil beneath to at least 1 foot (30 cm) down and roll a large thick sheet of polythene right under the ball of soil and roots. The plant is then lifted by the four corners of the sheet.

Stake the plant securely in its new position and water well in dry weather until well established. Where a lot of root has been left behind it may well be necessary to prune back the branches to compensate for this.

Transplanting a root-balled conifer

I have a sunless walled garden which is very damp. Nothing seems to grow. Is there anything I can plant which will brighten up this dreary spot? Part of the garden is overhung by a large tree.

GEOFFREY Had there not been a damp, shaded border on the north side of the house in this garden I would somehow have managed to contrive one.

You mention a tree without specifying what type. There are trees and trees – some like the oak are easy to garden under; others like the walnut, beech, sycamore, and horse-chestnut are well nigh impossible.

Under deciduous trees, bulbs which flower before the canopy of foliage develops are excellent. Snowdrops (*Galanthus*) winter aconites (*Eranthis*), hepatica, and wood anemones (*Anemone nemorosa* and varieties), American trout lily (*Erythronium* 'White Beauty'), mixed up with forget-me-nots (*Myosotis*), lenten roses (*Helleborus orientalis*) will make a notable contribution. For the summer, plant violas, busy lizzies (*Impatiens*), fuchsias and mimulus for a real blaze of colour.

There are several shrubs which revel in shade. Should the soil prove to be devoid of lime when you test it, then plant rhododendrons to form a permanent framework. *Acer japonicum* 'Aureum', *Berberis thunbergii* 'Aurea', *Viburnum davidii* – male and female so you get turquoise berries – and *Mahonia aquifolium* 'Apollo' will all be good value.

I would also feature ferns, which are so expressive of cool, moist shade. Ostrich plume (*Matteuccia*), hart's tongue (*Asplenium scolopendrium*) and several of the *Dryopteris* family are of real quality.

You must, however, provide all the above with humus-rich soil. Work in plenty of organic matter before planting. Any surface roots from the tree which could offer competition to the things you plant can be pruned out at the same time. Shade borders are assets, not liabilities.

There is a border at one end of my lawn which slopes up steeply. When it rains a lot the soil is washed down and the ground is very stony underneath. What sort of plants could I grow here – preferably low-maintenance as it is a difficult border to negotiate – which would help to bind the soil?

GEOFFREY A bank so steep that the soil washes off needs the slope, if possible, reduced in some way. A series of terraces supported by low retaining walls built of wood or stone would transform a difficult site into a number of easily worked beds. Alternatively, it should be possible with a few carefully contrived rock outcrops to take the steepness off the slope. Rock plants would then provide stability, colour and interest.

Should neither suggestion prove feasible, there is another solution. You can stop the soil erosion you are worried about by using plants with ground-hugging stems, especially those which root as they grow. *Cotoneaster adpressus*, *C. dammeri*, and *C. microphyllus* are first class for this purpose and so too are the heathers (*Erica*) – particularly the winter-flowering varieties. *Hypericum calycinum* (rose of Sharon) will quickly colonise the whole slope given the opportunity. Or you could try a mixed selection of ivies (*Hedera*) and allow them to intermingle and make a ground-stabilising tapestry. Two recently introduced ground-cover roses, 'Nozomi', and 'Snow Carpet', are worthy of consideration. And then there are the low-growing conifers, such as the prostrate forms of the common yew. *Taxus baccata* 'Repandens' and *T.b.*'Repens Aurea'. Among the prostrate forms of juniper are *Juniperus procumbens, J. communis depressa* and varieties of *J. horizontalis.*

Until the shrubs take over the available space, sow quick-growing annuals, such as nasturtiums and *Limnanthes douglasii* (poached egg flower). Also you can plant aubretia, phlox, alyssum and arabis for spring colour.

Could you recommend some attractive trees for small gardens? We have recently moved onto a housing estate where none of the gardens is very big and we are all afraid of planting ones which in time will outgrow their positions.

DAPHNE Trees to avoid in the situation you describe are the common forms of oak, ash, beech, sycamore, silver birch, lime and horse-chestnut which are more suitable for a forest or park. Unfortunately, small and slow-growing trees are usually much more expensive, and so people often opt for the cheaper alternatives in order to fill the garden up, sometimes with disastrous results.

My favourite tree for this type of position is *Acer pseudoplatanus* 'Brilliantissimum', a very slow-growing, mop-headed form of sycamore with leaves opening shrimp-pink, turning to bronze and then pale green.

For autumn colour, try *Crataegus prunifolia*, a form of hawthorn with large clusters of white flowers in June, followed by large, bright red 'haws' which are very popular with blackbirds and thrushes. The leaves turn a brilliant orange-scarlet, as do those of another tree attractive to birds, *Sorbus sargentiana*, a type of mountain ash which has red foliage in autumn.

Prunus 'Amanogawa' is probably the best form of flowering cherry for a confined space as it has very upright branches, so it takes up little space – although it can reach 20 feet (6 m) or more in height. *Prunus subhirtella* 'Autumnalis' is a small tree which can be in flower all winter if the weather is mild.

A tree which you can make any height you want depending on how it is trained is *Cotoneaster hybridus pendulus*. This is a prostrate shrub which, if tied to a cane of the chosen height, makes a small, evergreen weeping tree with white flowers and red berries.

Of course there are many more trees which would be equally suitable, but these are a start. I would not recommend planting any tree though, however diminutive, nearer to a property than 20 feet. If space is even tighter than this, an alternative is to train a small or medium-growing shrub on a single 'leg' four or five feet high. Some suitable subjects for this treatment are *Elaeagnus pungens* 'Aureo-maculata', *Syringa meyeri* 'Palibin' (a small form of lilac), holly (which can be pruned back), some spiraeas, flowering currant and dwarf forms of willow, e.g. *Salix lanata* and *Salix helvetica*.

Can you recommend some suitable climbers for a rustic pergola in full sun?

PETER   There are lots of good plants for this situation and a pretty red and white flowered runner bean called 'Painted Lady' will give a quick temporary cover and a crop. Where the soil is fertile then autumn-sown sweet peas will provide masses of fragrant flowers.

The woody climbers are the obvious permanent choice and climbing roses must be considered. Most of the perpetual flowering kinds such as 'Golden Showers', 'Handel' (cream edged deep pink), 'Compassion' (fragrant salmon-orange) and 'Danse du Feu' (scarlet) will all cover poles to 8 feet (2.2 m). Much stronger growing kinds such as 'Mermaid' (single yellow) and 'Seagull' (white) will grow up and over quite tall and long pergolas and arches. Plant some large-flowered clematis with the roses for even more colour.

The smaller-flowered *Clematis montana* provides fragrant blooms in May and growth which will swamp a pergola-covered walk. Golden hop (*Humulus lupulus* 'Aureus') has soft yellow leaves, grows fast and loves the sun. However, both lose their leaves in the depths of winter.

The large-leaved, brightly variegated ivy *Hedera colchica* 'Paddy's Pride' will thrive in sun. Plant it with *Clematis* 'Jackmanii Superba' and you will get a marvellous show of dark green and gold leaves plus deep purple clematis flowers.

Really large pergolas can be fully covered with Chinese gooseberry or kiwi fruit (*Actinidia deliciosa*) and vines (*Vitis*). One of the best vines for rich autumn leaf colour and small black fruit is *Vitis vinifera* 'Brandt', and *V. v.* 'Purpurea' has claret-coloured young leaves that turn purple. Place a silver-leaved weeping pear (*Pyrus salicifolia* 'Pendula') in front of this for a sparkling summer colour combination.

A sheltered warm trellis can be covered with *Solanum crispum* 'Glasnevin Variety' which has purple and yellow potato-like flowers in summer. The best pergola plant of all is the wisteria, but always pay the extra for grafted plants of named cultivars like *Wisteria floribunda* 'Macrobotrys'.

I have three clematis, 'Nellie Moser', 'Ville de Lyon' and 'The President'. Three weeks ago one of them started to wilt as though short of water. I watered it thoroughly but it didn't help. Now the other two are showing the same signs. What is happening?

BILL   It is a fact that nearly all varieties of clematis start into growth very early in spring. The pruning of clematis depends entirely on the flowering time of the variety. Those that flower towards the end of summer do so on wood produced the same year and should be pruned in early spring. If a variety flowers in very early spring that means it must be flowering on wood produced the previous year, and should be pruned after flowering time.

The majority of clematis wilt is caused by the fungal disease *Ascochyta clematidia*. I suggest you spray the plant and crown with benomyl or copper, drenching the soil around the root zone. Repeat the treatment 14 days later to protect new growth.

Frequently clematis whose top growth has wilted will recover if cut back to within 8 to 10 inches (20 to 25 cm) of soil level, and 3 to 4 inches (8 to 10 cm) of limy compost is applied over the root spread, with the stem pegged down horizontally into this new compost. By doing this you are encouraging a number of root systems, one from each node position, and the more root systems you have the less likely the plant is to suffer from wilt.

This is why it is policy when initially planting clematis to plant horizontally and not vertically. The ideal is to just cover each node position with alkaline soil, because apart from a root being produced from there, a new shoot will also appear.

How do you prune a wisteria to make it flower?

PETER   There are wisteria plants raised from seed, usually sold under the label *Wisteria sinensis*, and there are higher-priced grafted cultivars with names like *W. floribunda* 'Macrobotrys' and *W.* 'Purple Patches'. The seedlings are often very vigorous and slow to flower, while the named kinds are much more precocious and well worth the extra money.

Whichever type you have, if the growth is excessive and the flowers few or non-existent, two prunings will help to produce flower buds. First, pinch out with the thumbnail the growing tip of *all* the young shoots coming from the main stem or stems once they are 6 inches (15 cm) or so long. If the stem has become too tough to pinch out in this way, it has been left too long. Regrowth will also need to be pinched back.

On large plants this will be quite a task but if pursued the growth will be checked and once the plant has been pruned to flower it should continue flowering every year.

After the repeated summer pruning, all the woody side-shoots, or spurs as they are called, should be pruned even harder back with secateurs in winter. At this time the short, six-month-old stems should be pruned back to two buds. With plants that produce a good set of plump flower buds, winter pruning may not be necessary.

Once again, as with many non-flowering, vigorous-growing shrubs, do not feed except perhaps to apply a little sulphate of potash in spring.

Wisteria makes a very good tub plant and can also be trained up a single stem to form a very pretty, small weeping tree. Growing a plant in a large tub restricts the roots and this will help to stimulate earlier flowering. Once it is flowering well the wisteria can be taken from the tub and planted in the permanent position. Wisterias do not take kindly to being dug up and transplanted, however; even if they survive this they sometimes take a full year before breaking into new growth.

> *I am erecting a new fence which will be north-facing. What climbers would you suggest to give colour throughout the year? Also, what is the most effective climber for covering completely an unsightly garage?*

PETER   There are few climbers that are attractive year round as well as free-flowering. One of the best approaches is a dual planting of the green and gold-leaved ivy *Hedera helix* 'Goldheart' and the rich purple-flowered *Clematis* 'Jackmanii Superba'. The thin stems of the clematis twine up among the small variegated ivy leaves and are hidden when leafless and unattractive in winter.

A number of the clematis, including 'Nelly Moser' and 'Bee's Jubilee', are more brightly coloured out of direct sunlight. Another possible combination is yellow winter-flowering jasmine – *Jasminum nudiflorum* – and one of the Virgina creepers (*Parthenocissus*).

All these plants are self-clinging and twining, but there are free-standing shrubs too which can be planted against north-facing fences. Cotoneaster and firethorn (*Pyracantha*) are two good examples. You could also train such fruiting plants as redcurrants and morello cherry in this position.

Cover an unsightly garage with the ivies for the best evergreen cover. If you do not mind bare stems in winter then the deciduous mile-a-minute or Russian vine (*Polygonum baldschuanicum*) is one of the most rampant climbers and scramblers of all. Each year in late summer it is covered in white, frothy flowers. Quite honestly, the polygonum is too gross for me and I would prefer one of the ever-green ivies or deciduous *Parthenocissus tricuspidata* 'Veitchii' to cover ugly buildings. When planting these strong climbers always leave them trailing along the ground. They become established much quicker this way and climb up the fence or wall faster when left to their own devices, rather than having the young shoots tied upright to canes or wires.

None of the plants mentioned is fragrant and one of the best climbers for north-facing positions, with rapid covering-growth and scented, small pink flowers in May, is *Clematis montana* 'Elizabeth'. It is only semi-evergreen.

How do I eradicate couch grass from a rockery?

GEOFFREY At the risk of being called a Jeremiah, my answer is: Not without difficulty. There is a chemical with the trade name of Weed-out which can be sprayed onto the young couch when it has five or six leaves showing. The active agent is reported to be specific to couch and other grass-type plants and should, therefore, not harm broad-leaved plants in the rock garden. If I sound a trifle dubious, the reason is that excessive use of chemicals has never been a part of my routine garden practice. Also, when I tried the chemical on a couch-infested rock garden it failed to give a complete kill. Apparently, heavy infestation may require repeat applications for full eradication.

I believe the most effective way of getting rid of couch grass, and refurbishing the rock garden at the same time, would be to strip the whole lot down. I had to do this with a 3-year-old limestone-based rock garden, so you will appreciate how daunting the task was.

First remove all the shrubs – taking care not to damage the roots more than necessary – and 'heel' them in. Burying the roots in moist peat in a shaded corner of the garden is one method. They can be safely left then for six months or more.

All the stone can then be removed to one side, leaving the weed-infested area clear for treatment. I took the easy way out and used sodium chlorate – a total weedkiller which persists in the soil for six months. By applying the chemical in autumn (October in my case), the soil was clean for rebuilding to begin the following May. I've heard that where the weed is particularly well established the best long-term control is with dichlobenil (Casoron G4), but replanting will not be possible for 12 months.

You could use the less persistent weedkiller, glyphosate (Tumbleweed). The snag is that glyphosate is not that effective as it is poorly translocated in this weed. The best approach is to wet the foliage throughly with glyphosate every four weeks until the weed is controlled, or use the spot treatment gel where it is close to cultivated plants.

I have a small rockery with alpine phlox and dianthus which have become very straggly. Should I cut them back?

GEOFFREY Trimming back most varieties of *Phlox douglasii* and *P. subulata* after flowering is necessary to keep them neat and well flowered.

Pruning on a regular basis will do no harm but drastic cutting back, I find, can be detrimental. As a precaution take some cuttings of young growths in spring, root them in sand and then risk hard pruning.

Once dianthus have become very straggly they are best dug out and replaced with young stock raised from cuttings. Do plant into fresh soil. Once you have cuttings rooted, try hard pruning, though in my experience this rarely results in a rejuvenated plant – merely a dead one.

I have a big stone sink about six inches (15 cm) deep and I would like to plant alpines in it. What compost should I use and could you give me some ideas for suitable subjects?

GEOFFREY A stone sink could become a family heirloom, like grandma's dining-room table.

Before filling the sink with compost, make sure there is a drainage-hole in the bottom – alpine plants detest sitting with their roots in a bog, so all excess water needs to filter away quickly. Cover the hole with a piece of perforated zinc or pieces of clay plant-pot. Next put in a layer of roughage; coarse leaf-mould, peat or loam tailings are the best, though bark is another I am trying.

The compost is made up of 5 parts by bulk of John Innes compost mixed with 1 part of sharp sand. Which grade of John Innes depends on the type of plant; No. 2 is a good all-rounder, suiting most plants.

When the trough is filled with compost, try to find just one or two moss-encrusted pieces of stone with which to landscape and break up the level surface.

The number and variety of alpine plants suitable for growing in troughs is bewildering. A trough in my garden is planted entirely with 'cushion' saxifrages (*Kabschia*). There are four varieties – *Saxifraga burseriana* 'Gloria', *S.* 'Cranbourne', *S.* x *jenkinsae*, and *S.* 'Faldonside'. All flower outdoors in late winter and offer silvered cushions of foliage thereafter. You can achieve the same year-round effect by planting different varieties of house leek (*Sempervivum*).

I would suggest trying the birdseye primrose (*Primula farinosa*) and the spring gentian (*Gentiana verna*). Both of these are native and neat.

Also flowering in spring is *Aethionema grandiflora, Aubreta* 'Red Carpet' (cut back after flowering to keep it neat) and *Armeria caespitosa* 'Bevan's Variety'.

For summer, I would suggest *Campanula aucheri, C. pusilla* and any other of the less invasive alpine *Campanula* species. You could plant one of the *Phlox douglasii* varieties, but trim hard after flowering.

For autumn and winter flowers, I would recommend *Penstemon pinifolius, Cyclamen hederifolium (C. napolitanum)* and *C. coum.*

Try also some bulbs. Dwarf narcissus, tulips and crocus are excellent for troughs on a temporary basis.

Though a depth of 6 inches (15 cm) allows only limited space for root development there are conifers slow-growing enough to function for several years before growing too large for your trough. I would recommend the spire-shaped *Juniperus communis* 'Compressa', or *Chamaecyparis lawsoniana* 'Minima Aurea' which is like a golden-yellow bun.

Can blanketweed be eliminated? My pond is solid with it.

PETER   While I have no pond in my own garden, this is a problem I am often asked about. The standard answer is to remove blanketweed manually, twisting the head of a rake through the water to gather up strands and pull it out. But be careful to avoid puncturing butyl and plastic pool liners with such tools.

There are chemicals that can be added to the water to remove green algae and rapidly clear the water. They tend to be short-lived, however, and while the chemicals do no harm to fish, in very weedy water the killed-off green matter rots and this rotting process can release chemicals harmful to fish.

Long-term cultural methods are best and here you need to keep the amount of plant food in the water down and encourage leaf cover to block out light. Repeatedly changing the water is likely to do more harm than good. A good spread of broad water lily leaves certainly blocks out light and helps to reduce blanketweed growth. Similarly, fairy moss (*Azolla*) will carpet the water surface, but this can grow very rapidly in summer and completely hide the fish from view.

It has often occurred to me that the black polythene mulch used to smother weeds in soil could be used on ponds. Floated on a section of the water surface for ten days or so in summer, it would block out light and kill blanketweed and green algae. I asked aquatic specialist David Everett of Anglo Aquarian about this and he tells me German fish breeders use black polythene to control weed growth in their lagoons. So if you can float some black polythene over the surface of part of your pond, it might do the trick. You will of course have to cut holes in it to allow the water lily and other desired aquatic plant leaves to get the light.

Cloudy water is quickly cleared with a few drops of a coagulant called Greenaway.

How do you look after a pond in winter?

BILL   At first sight of the question of what to do with a garden pond in winter, I considered my own masterly inactivity. Then after more consideration, I realised that there are essentials to keep the pond in a satisfactory state of natural balance for the plants and the fish therein.

The first requirement is to think about the autumn, and to arrange some two foot high fine-mesh Netlon, or something similar, around the pond in a vertical fashion. This is to stop leaves blowing into the pond and fouling the water.

Are there any herons in the neighbourhood? If there are, it may be necessary to put netting over the pond, if that is feasible. Herons swoop vertically onto fish in ponds and off they fly with that beautiful, slow, powerful wing-beat.

It is good policy to remove decaying aquatic vegetation, because as decay takes place gases are given off which may be trapped under ice, much to the detriment of fish life.

When frost is forecast it pays to float a beach ball or two on the surface before it becomes frozen, and this will satisfactorily take care of the expansion and contraction of the freezing of the water, and importantly allow sufficient oxygen to reach the fish. Ponds with electrical pumps which keep the water on the move will usually allow oxygen movement also. When very hard frosts are threatened, it pays to cover the pump mechanics with sacking or old clothing, to reduce the possibility of a freeze-up and later rupture of the pump. You may want to use one of the many safe electrical pool heaters that are on the market, but remember that all electrical appliances must be installed by a competent electrician. If there are fish in the pond, never ever break the ice with a sharp blow.

We have just moved and the new garden is very boggy. What kind of plants would do well under such conditions?

DAPHNE   If you don't want to go to the trouble and expense of draining your garden, there are many plants which look good and do well under boggy conditions. I would suggest that you keep any lawn area down to a minimum as it will be difficult to keep it in first-class order if it is badly drained.

That beautiful, meadowsweet-like plant, the astilbe, would always be my first choice. It has feathery plumes of flowers ranging in colour from pure white to deep red, and there are heights among the different varieties to suit any position. For something similar but much taller there is *Aruncus sylvester* (*A. dioicus*), and there is also the true meadowsweet family (*Filipendula*).

Hostas appreciate moisture at the roots and there is a tremendous choice available – green- or glaucous-leaved, variegated, tall, dwarf, white flowers or purple, many being delightfully scented.

There are many irises which need moist conditions, such as the many forms of *Iris sibirica*, *I. kaempferi* (which needs a lime-free soil) and the yellow flag, *I. pseudacorus*.

A plant which is likely to become popular is *Houttuynia cordata* 'Chameleon', with multi-coloured leaves. This is useful for the front of a border, but, if you want something striking for the back, then the large parasol-leaved rodgersias are for you. Another flamboyant plant is the huge ornamental rhubarb (*Rheum*).

No collection of moisture-loving plants would be complete without the marsh marigold, *Caltha palustris*, or the buttercup family (*Ranunculus*). And I would always include some of the moisture-happy candelabra primulas like *Primula bulleyana*, *P. pulverulenta* and *P. japonica*.

Most bog-garden herbaceous perennials die down in winter, so it is a good idea to include some shrubs suitable for this kind of situation, for example the red-stemmed dogwood *Cornus alba*, or its variegated forms, and some of the willows which have coloured bark, like the bronze-stemmed *Salix fargesii*, *S. daphnoides* (violet willow) and *S. alba* 'Chermesina' (scarlet willow), to give winter interest. Left unpruned these shrubs will soon make very big bushes, but, as the best coloured bark is on the young wood, the best effect is obtained by cutting them down to ground level every other year, which will also keep them within bounds.

I have had a peony in the garden for six years and it refuses to flower. I realise it takes some time for them to settle down after being moved but I had expected results before now.

PETER   While peonies do not take kindly to transplanting they can be moved satisfactorily and should be flowering again in much less than six years. The best time to lift, divide and transplant is when the foliage has died down from late summer. Container-grown plants can of course be planted any time the soil is neither frozen nor waterlogged.

A sunny or semi-shaded position is suitable and the soil should be free-draining but have plenty of well rotted garden compost, manure or peat dug in to hold moisture in summer. Heavy clay soils, somewhat water-logged in winter, lacking organic matter and cracking in summer, are likely to delay flowering, as may dense shade.

Peonies should not be planted too deep, and covering the crowns with too much soil is the most common cause of non-flowering. The crowns – thick fleshy roots – of these plants should be covered with no more than 1 inch (2.5 cm) of soil.

Mulching the crowns each spring with well-rotted compost, coupled with watering in dry weather, will improve growth and flowering.

If the flower buds form but instead of opening turn black and die, the disease botrytis should be suspected. Watering the crowns when new growth forms in early spring with systemic fungicide and spraying the leaves twice at fortnightly intervals will control this disease. Very severe attacks may require the cutting back of old stems, careful raking away of surface soil and replacing with fresh soil as well as the fungicide treatment.

Late spring frost can occasionally cause damage to peony buds and prevent flowering for a year.

How do you tidy up a pampas grass after flowering? What can I do to encourage it to produce more plumes next year as this year it only had two?

BILL   Pampas grass (*Cortaderia selloana*), a South-American native, is well known as a very fine plant for isolated positions on lawns. But in selecting a site it is important to take account of the very sharp, file-like leaf edges. The leaves are really quite fearsome, so do not plant a pampas anywhere near a path.

The plant will grow in most soils but a deep, well-drained loam is the best. A vital planting consideration, however, is that the position must be in full sun to produce the best plumes.

The silky plumes of the female plants are much more beautiful than those of the male, and very considerable variation occurs in seedlings of habit, period of flowering and size of panicle.

Seedlings will take longer to produce plumes than named varieties, so if growing from seed always choose those from a parent plant which is known to produce plumes early in life.

For indoor decoration the plumes should be cut just as the panicles are emerging, and are best dried in the sun for two or three days and then laid on a shelf in the garage or in the shade in the greenhouse, until the stems are quite dry. If they are left too long in such a position the spikelets are apt to be shed and the beauty lost.

In early spring the plants can be trimmed with shears to remove the dead foliage which inevitably accumulates. It used to be considered good practice to put some dry hay or straw between the old leaves in early March and to have a quick burn. This helped to clean the plant up and to destroy some pests, but unless it is done correctly there can be damage to young growths that may be emerging.

In summary, to produce the best plumes you need a rich soil, no disturbance, heavy compost dressings each early spring, plus a handful or two of Growmore fertiliser. And ideally you need a female as opposed to a male plant. So you will gather pampas is unlike the peacock. In the first the female is the most attractive, in the second the male is the one who struts and displays his finery.

Can an overgrown Leyland cypress hedge be cut back severely?
Mine has got out of hand, and I want to halve its height to six
feet (2 m) and reduce the width. Is it possible to use the prunings
as cuttings?

BILL   It is my opinion that the very quick-growing hybrid x *Cupressocyparis leylandii* (*Cupressus macrocarpa* x *Chamaecyparis nootkatensis*) has been over-planted this last 25 years, and many a gardener is now suffering from its vigour.

Leyland cypress is a marvellous subject for providing a quick screen but is sometimes planted in the wrong position, and when it finds itself happy, in reasonable soil, it sets off for the heavens. Unless it is controlled by spring clipping to check further upward and excessive side-growth, in a few years the owner will need extension ladders plus danger money.

I gather you want to reduce yours to half its present height, to 6 feet (2 m), and to reduce its width. The best time to do any such hard pruning is at the onset of growth, and certainly not when growth is stopping in the autumn. So hard prune in mid- to late March, and seeing that you want the hedge to finish at 6 feet (2 m), I suggest you cut it back then to 4 feet (120 cm). It is advisable to top-dress the root spread with 3 to 4 inches (8 to 10 cm) of very old garden compost, and to give a handful or two of Growmore fertiliser to each tree. You will then find very quick new growth will be produced.

I would expect if you did cut back hard to 4 feet (120 cm) it will be up to 6 feet (2 m) by July/August, and then you should keep it trimmed at the top and the sides. It never pays to allow a cupressus of any variety to get too dense because light is then excluded from the central growths which inevitably turn brown.

So with Leyland cypress you keep it regularly pruned, and do not over-feed. In fact you treat it like the old country maxim 'The wife, the dog, the walnut tree – the harder you beat them, the better they be'.

Hard pruning a Leyland cypress hedge in spring to allow later growth

I am thinking of making a conifer and heather bed. I would like suggestions for slow-growing conifers of various colours and heathers for year-round interest. I have tested the soil and find the pH is about 7.

GEOFFREY To enable you to be able to choose from the whole range of heathers – *Calluna* and *Erica* – the soil needs to be lime-free (acid). With a pH reading of 7 your soil is neutral, so a heavy dressing of peat would be sufficient to ensure the acid root-run heathers prefer.

There is almost an infinite variety of conifers to choose from, though you might like to consider the following which all grow well in my garden: *Thuja orientalis* 'Aurea Nana' (yellow), *Taxus baccata* 'Standishii' (yellow), *Pinus mugo* 'Mops' (green), *Picea pungens* 'Globosa' (silver), *Chamaecyparis obtusa* 'Nana Gracilis' (green), *Juniperus* x *media* 'Old Gold' (gold). Just a word of warning – do not let over-vigorous heathers swamp the conifers in the early stages.

Now for the heathers and a point to remember when planting: bury the roots so the bases of the stems are covered, and then add a moisture-conserving top dressing of peat for the stems to root into.

Calluna vulgaris varieties, flowering August to November: 'Golden Feather' (golden-yellow foliage), 'H. E. Beale' (double pink flowers), 'Silver Knight' (silver foliage, pink flowers).

Erica herbacea (E. carnea) varieties, winter-flowering: 'Myretoun Ruby' (ruby-red), 'Springwood White' (white).

E. darleyensis, winter-flowering: 'Arthur Johnson' (rose-pink), 'Silberschmelze' (white).

E. erigena (*E. mediterranea*), spring-flowering: 'Brightness' (purple-red), 'W. T. Rackliff' (white).

E. vagans (Cornish heath), summer-flowering: 'Mrs D. F. Maxwell' (rose-cerise), 'Lyonesse' (white).

E. cinerea (which can be a temperamental summer-flowering species): 'C. D. Eason' (red-pink), 'Fiddlers Gold' (yellow foliage and lilac-pink flowers), 'White Dale' (white).

The above is a useful selection for all-the-year-round interest, but you can add to these as fancy dictates.

(The *Erica herbacea*, *E. darleyensis* and *E. erigena* varieties are to some extent lime-tolerant.)

Heather, showing correct depth for planting

> *Can certain bedding plants, e.g. geraniums, fuchsias, fibrous-rooted begonias and Cineraria maritima be kept from year to year without a greenhouse?*

PETER   The simple reply here is yes! But different plants need different treatments. Grey-leaved *Cineraria maritima* will survive outside for several winters in mild areas. For most of us these plants will need dry peat heaped around the base of the stem and straw or dry grass wrapped around the foliage. If it works, fine, but quite honestly it is safer to raise new plants from seed.

The fibrous-rooted *Begonia semperflorens* is different; one touch of a frost and they're dead. Lift them carefully in September before the chance of frost and they make marvellous winter-flowering house plants. The 5¹/₂ inch (13 cm) half-pots that chrysanthemums are grown in are ideal for these begonias and after a winter indoors they can be planted in the garden again. Just cut them back if they get too tall.

Fuchsias, zonal and ivy-leaved geraniums, *Pelargonium zonale* and *P. peltatum*, are best renewed by rooting cuttings in late summer and overwintering these vigorous young plants indoors. Many people, however, want to keep the one-year-old and older plants. To do this, stop watering in late September; this ripens and hardens the stems. A lot of the older leaves will then yellow and fall.

Before a really hard frost, cut off the soft green tips and bury the whole plant – roots still intact in the pot of compost or big ball of soil – in dry peat. You can dig a hole in a free-draining area in the garden or greenhouse border soil, place the plants on their sides, cover with dry peat and then with a layer of soil. Frost seldom reaches down

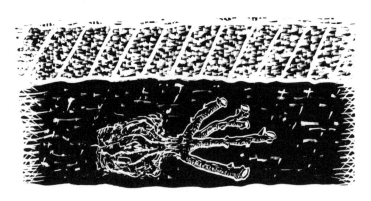

Fuchsia, pruned back and covered with dry peat and a layer of soil

through 6 inches (15 cm) of soil. Alternatively, place the plants in a large box and surround with dry peat and keep them in a shed or garage. Frost again will seldom penetrate through 6 inches (15 cm) of dry peat in a shed.

I want to grow really good sweet peas. What is the best way to go about it?

BILL   First of all comes the choice of varieties, which to me means picking those colours that I like, providing they are also highly scented.

The sweet pea is quite hardy but not fully, and probably the best time to sow is in late September, and to overwinter the seedlings in a cold frame or unheated greenhouse. The plants must have plenty of ventilation during the winter, and only need the protection of a couple of sheets of newspaper in very, very hard weather. In good districts sweet peas can be sown direct outdoors in autumn, providing the plants are covered with cloches during the worst of the wether, and because they then do not need transplanting, early flowers will be produced.

Another fine way of growing sweet peas is to sow in autumn in large pots, again overwintering in a cold greenhouse, and allow them to flower in the greenhouse.

It is important with most varieties that the initial leader growth produced from the seed is pinched so that side-shoots are produced, and these are the ones that carry the flowers.

Most professional sweet pea growers treat the sweet pea seeds with a fungicidal seed dressing before sowing, but they never recommend soaking the seeds in water. It is a fact that the blue and maroon shades have very hard seeds, and germination can be accelerated by chipping the seed coat with a penknife on the side away from the 'eye'.

The position in the garden must be well drained, it must be in full sun, and there should be some very old manure or very old garden compost forked in down below, ideally during winter. On top of the manure or compost sprinkle a handful of superphosphate of lime per yard (m) run, then cover with 3 to 4 inches (8 to 10 cm) of soil and mark the manured position with sticks so that you sow or plant directly on that position in spring. The sweet peas will need some support, which could be canes, string or plastic netting, and should be securely fixed.

There should be regular liquid feeding during the growing season, which is applied in the late evening, and it must be a balanced feed which also contains necessary trace elements such as iron, magnesium and boron.

Last year, none of my daffodil bulbs had any flowers. There were plenty of leaves, but some of them looked rather thin. What's gone wrong?

GEOFFREY Like any other plants which grow in our gardens daffodils, and all the other types of narcissus, need feeding. Then after a few years – how many depends on the distance apart they were planted in the first place – the bulbs spread by offsets to become overcrowded. Lift the bulbs when the foliage dies back and let them dry off so they can be safely stored until the soil has been refurbished ready for replanting in September.

Dress the soil with well-rotted compost, leaf-mould, composted bark, peat, even manure which has stood for two years in the stack. Never ever use fresh manure in soil which is intended to grow daffodils. Dig in the organic dressing, then, just prior to planting, rake in a dressing of bonemeal at the rate of 2 oz per sq yard (70 gm per sq m). You can either replant the old bulbs or, as I prefer, select the best of the old and buy a selection of new bulbs to make sure there is a good display of flowers.

Do not cut down the foliage of daffodils until at least eight weeks after the flowers fade. Also, in my experience, daffodil bulbs whether in borders or under grass, need to be planted at least 6 inches (15 cm) deep.

There are certain pests and diseases which attack daffodils. One of these is stem eel worm which causes soft bulbs and poor growth. Infected plants should be lifted and destroyed. *Do not* replant into infected soil. Plants affected by narcissus fly have distorted leaves and their bulbs are eaten by the maggot-like larvae. Again, they should be lifted and destroyed. If your daffodils have scorched and yellowing leaves the problem could be caused by a virus and they should be sprayed in order to control the disease-spreading aphis. The most serious disease attacking daffodils is basal rot which results in yellowing of leaf tips. Good husbandry – regular feeding, lifting and dividing of overcrowded bulbs – is the best control. However, as you do not mention distortion, yellowing or rotting of the foliage, I am assuming the trouble is starvation.

What are you supposed to do with double begonias, dahlias and gladioli when they have finished flowering?

BILL   Most, but not all, double begonia varieties produce stem-tubers. The begonia tuber contains stored food material in a kind of subterranean stem which has a leathery skin. The 'normal', large-flowered, double begonias are deciduous. The foliage dies down in November or so, and the idea is to store the dormant tubers cool and dry during the winter. This tuber is always slightly saucer-shaped and is planted as you would position a saucer, with the hollow or concave side upwards. Dusting the tubers with powdered sulphur before storing in dry sand is a wise precaution, and the position must be cool but frost-free. As sulphur is now difficult to obtain, benomyl powder can be used instead.

The same can be said of the tuberous roots of the dahlia. They, too, have to be stored dry and cool and be coated with sulphur or benomyl powder. They should be stored upright so that the portion of dead stem is vertical. In mild parts of the country some dahlias can be safely left in the ground over winter and will mostly get through safely, but it is considered wise to lift and label tubers each winter and to store them in a dry and cool place.

The gladiolus produces a corm and although a corm may look like a bulb it is in fact different. A corm consists of a solid, swollen stem on which are sheathing scale-like leaves. On the surface of the corm are one or two buds from which a new plant will grow. True bulbs, e.g. onion, daffodil, contain a small disc-like stem at the base from which arises the leaf bases of last year's foliage, swollen with food material.

Storing tuberous-rooted begonias and dahlia tubers

The gladiolus corm is fairly frost-tender, yet in many martime districts it will get through the winter quite safely when left undisturbed outdoors. Nevertheless, I think it is safer to lift, dry off, store cool and dry, and replant in spring.

◇

How do you pot and care for hyacinth bulbs, please? You talk of 'prepared bulbs'; what exactly is meant by this?

DAPHNE 'Prepared' bulbs are specially treated by the grower to ensure that they flower early when potted-up for home decoration. If you want your hyacinths in flower at Christmas they should be planted no later than September.

Hyacinth bulbs are usually potted up in bulb fibre, which contains charcoal to keep the compost 'sweet'; this is especially important if the bowl has no drainage holes. General purpose peat-based compost can be used instead, however, if care is taken with the watering. Never use ordinary garden soil which will contain pests and diseases and is likely to become waterlogged.

Place a layer of bulb fibre or compost in the bottom of the bowl, and position the hyacinth bulbs on this so they do not touch each other or the sides of the bowl. Add more fibre, firming it *gently* round the bulbs, until the tops are just sticking out and there is about half an inch between the surface of the fibre or compost and the top of the bowl. The fibre should be moist, but not wet.

The planted bowl must then be put in a cool, dark place for about 6 to 10 weeks so that the bulbs can produce a strong root system. If you haven't a suitable spot in the garden where the bowl can be

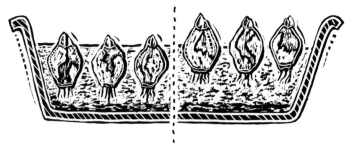

Alternative methods for planting hyacinth bulbs – planting them higher up is less likely to cause rotting through overwatering but the bulbs are less stable in the bowl

covered over with peat, a cool, dark cupboard will do, or put it in a bag in an unheated garage or shed, but it is very important that the bulbs are kept cold at this stage or the flowers will not develop properly.

The bowl is ready to be brought into the light when about 1 inch (2.5 cm) of top growth is showing. The bulbs should be given a cool, shady position at first, gradually moving them into a light place but still keeping them cool. When the colour is beginning to show on the flowers they can be put in a warmer room if desired, but the display will last longer given cool conditions.

Don't allow the compost to dry out, but be careful not to over-water it if there are no drainage holes in the bowl. When the flowers have faded, if you cut them off, leaving the stalks on the bulbs, and continue to water and feed the leaves with a houseplant fertiliser you will be able to plant the bulbs in the garden when the weather has warmed up, but they won't be suitable for indoor cultivation again.

Are there any plants hardy enough to survive the winter if planted in a hanging basket on a sheltered wall?

BILL   There are many subjects which would be hardy in a hanging basket left outdoors, and they include some of the sedums, saxifrages, the pasque flower (*Pulsatilla vulgaris*), various dwarf primulas, dwarf potentillas, dwarf phlox, aubrietia, pink arabis, the 'Universal' strain of winter-flowering pansies, edelweiss (*Leontopodium alpinum*), lewisia, dwarf rock geranium, rock-rose, *Draba aizoides*, dwarf dianthus, dwarf campanula, dwarf asters, thrift (*Armeria*), dwarf astilbe, dwarf arenaria, dwarf perennial alyssum, various small-leaved variegated ivies, lesser periwinkle (*Vinca minor*) and dwarf veronica.

The problem with planting a hanging basket with 'permanent' subjects is the fact that in a year or two some will outgrow and smother the less dominant kinds. So there will always be an imbalance which will need to be controlled by pruning, or elimination. There is also the problem of feeding and soil replacement. When you are growing subjects in pots it is usual to repot in larger pots using fresh compost perhaps every couple of years, and with a hanging basket there must be an attempt to replace or top up the compost or the subjects will languish.

Another difficulty is watering the plants in spring and summer when growth will be active and transpiration considerable. It is best to have the hanging basket on a pulley so that you can let it down to an easy watering height. There are special watering devices which help the process. In winter, of course, little will be required, though if the plants are evergreen some water will be required or there will be dehydration. The basket should be moved to a position still outdoors but where the soil will not freeze.

An easy way of watering during the summer is to put three or four ice cubes on top of the compost. They will gradually melt and progressively and satisfactorily water the subjects.

I wish to grow shrubs in tubs to brighten up the walls of my bungalow. Can you advise me how to calculate the size of tub in relation to the shrub, and what subjects would be most successful?

DAPHNE   Most garden plants can be grown satisfactorily in tubs, providing the right size of container and the right compost are used. Always use as large a tub as you can – at least 18 inches (46 cm) square or in diameter by the same depth – or the roots will become very restricted. For this kind of permanent planting a soil-based potting compost is best – I use John Innes No. 3.

The type of plants you choose is really a matter of personal preference once you've got the conditions right, but, because they are in containers, I feel that evergreen shrubs probably look better. However I know many people who grow climbing roses in this way and the summer effect is good, although they look rather boring in winter. If you do want roses, choose the less rampant ones, like the yellow-and-red 'Joseph's Coat', red 'Aloha' or some of the more lax-growing shrub roses.

Pyracantha, cotoneaster, ceanothus, escallonia and variegated forms of ivy all grow well in containers and can be pruned to shape. True climbers, like honeysuckle, wisteria, vines (*Vitis*), clematis, actinidia and campsis seem to look even more untidy when out of flower as the tub tends to draw attention to them, so I usually recommend planting another, smaller and more attractive shrub, like for example, variegated euonymus, at the base.

As it is a bungalow we are talking about, the walls won't be very high, so virtually any shrub, elevated 18 inches (46 cm) as it will be, will probably do the job. Camellias are especially suitable as they can be grown in containers of lime-free compost when often ordinary garden soil is unsuitable because of being too alkaline.

Tubs against walls tend to get very dry and can even need regular watering in winter. In summer, a liquid fertiliser can be added to the water according to the manufacturer's instructions. Ericaceous plants like camellias must be watered with soft water, or given an annual treatment with sequestrene to prevent lime-induced chlorosis, which shows itself as a yellowing of the leaves.

Could you suggest plants to give colour all the year round in tubs in our west-facing patio? What compost should be used and should this be renewed annually, or is there some method of rejuvenating it?

DAPHNE   First, a word of advice about the kind of tubs being used. Although it's tempting to stock up with cheap, thin plastic ones, it's false economy as they easily freeze solid in winter, and become quite brittle when constantly exposed to the rays of the sun. You are far better to invest in one or two really solid stone, imitation stone or well constructed timber ones, adding to these when funds allow.

The compost to use really depends on what you want to grow in your tubs. The most widely used plants for patio decoration are bedding plants – pelargoniums, fuchsias, French marigolds, ageratums, salvias and the like for summer, replaced with winter-flowering pansies, polyanthus and spring-flowering bulbs for the months between October and May. If this is the kind of thing that interests you, then a lightweight, peat-based potting compost will do, but this needs to be replaced annually. It can be used in the garden as a mulch afterwards.

However, you can achieve year-round colour by using attractive-leaved shrubs instead of bedding plants. Ones I've found particularly satisfactory in a west-facing position are *Elaeagnus pungens* 'Aureo-Maculata', *Choisya ternata* 'Sundance', variegated yucca, dwarf hebes, especially the grey-leaved and golden 'whipcord' varieties, dwarf and medium-growing conifers and *Azalea japonica* – it can be rather too hot for many other types of rhododendron. Miniature roses will also give useful summer colour, but they need to be mixed with spring bulbs to liven up the planting at the beginning of the year. For these more permanent subjects, a soil-based compost is desirable. John Innes No. 3 compost will contain enough nutrients for the first season, but a liquid fertiliser should be given about once a fortnight in summer in subsequent years. Once the shrubs have reached a good size, remove the top couple of inches of compost annually and replace it with fresh John Innes No. 3.

Don't forget to water adequately in summer – every day in dry spells, and for large, well-established plants.

FRUIT & VEGETABLES

GROWING SOMETHING THAT YOU CAN EAT MUST surely be the most sensible aspect of gardening. Everything else may be summed up as mere decoration, but fruit and veg are essentials.

I recently planted lettuces, cauliflowers and Brussels sprouts and, having spent a long time preparing the soil, I had high hopes of speedy results. Now, I should perhaps point out that gardening is for me a haphazard pursuit. Visits to the vegetable patch are none too frequent, and when I next had occasion to peer into this particular corner an astonishing sight met my eyes.

Instead of the expected rows of green goodies, a large collection of triffids appeared to have taken up residence. Every plant seemed to be a lot bigger than predicted, and most looked nothing like the picture on the packet. (And there is nothing more disconcerting for us non-gardeners.) I could barely make out the lettuces, which resembled pagodas, having grown upwards in tiers to a height of two feet. It was some weeks later that Peter Seabrook explained about lettuces 'bolting' to me. Now it may seem daft, but I had somehow expected them to stop when they reached the right size.

On the programme, we always get calls about 'club root' and 'blossom end rot', and I often think how powerful they would be as words of insult.

Imagine the scene down at the local. The froth on your pint has just been blown in your face, and the neanderthal who happens to have taken against you is about to crush your cheese and onions. As the rest of the pub falls silent, you draw yourself up level with his chest and say contemptuously: 'Just the kind of thing I'd expect from a club root like you. Well, I just hope your blossom end rots, that's all!'

Then you run for the door . . .

JOHN THIRLWELL

I have a four-year-old 'Black Hamburg' grape vine planted against a west-facing fence. Last year the leaves, and what little fruit there was, were covered in a white, mouldy substance. I also noticed the bark had many crustacean-like lumps on it. This year there is an enormous crop of grapes but they are not growing. What can I do to improve the situation?

GEOFFREY From your description I would suspect the white mould is an indication that your vine is infected with the fungus called powdery mildew. The first symptoms show as patches on the under-sides of leaves. I am not surprised the grapes failed to develop for the disease is serious.

Two or three applications at 14-day intervals of the systemic fungicide benomyl or a mixture containing bupirimate is a thorough way of controlling this disease. Also three or four applications of sulphur dust is an effective remedy, if you can get it, and as your vine is growing outdoors there should be no chemical damage.

The crustacean-like lumps offer a fairly accurate description of scale insect, possibly mussel scale, although woolly vine scale can also attack grapes outdoors. The simplest and most effective control is to paint the colonies with a tar acid or tar oil wash in December or January. The vines must be completely dormant, and do apply the wash carefully to avoid risk of damage to plants growing near by.

Pests and diseases duly mastered, correct pruning, watering and feeding will be in your control. Unfortunately the weather is totally outside your authority and the 'Black Hamburg' grape would be better suited to growing in a greenhouse. An outdoor variety such as 'Siegerrebe' or 'Noir Hatif de Marseilles' might have been a more suitable choice.

We planted a new pear tree last year and this year it had one pear on it. Could you give us some idea of what to do next – pruning and spraying?

BILL It is a fact that many pears are self-sterile, so you need a compatible variety in your own or a nearby garden before you can expect regular crops. Nevertheless, your pear has only been in a year and it should not have been allowed to crop at all until established.

The idea with most hard fruits, which would include pears, apples, plums, gages, damsons, peaches, nectarines and apricots, is to choose if possible a self-fertile variety, or if not to have two or more varieties that are compatible, and to allow them to establish a good root and branch system before they are asked to bear the additional strain of setting, swelling and ripening a crop.

For reliable control of aphid, winter moth, capsid sucker, codling and tortrix moth, scab and mildew, all varieties of pears – and all other deciduous fruit trees – should be sprayed at bud burst, petal fall and at the early and late fruitlet stages with a combined insecticide and fungicide.

The important thing to remember about pruning is that if you prune hard in winter you inevitably produce a lot of new growth in spring, which will need to be reduced, and will not flower that year. On the other hand, if you prune in mid-July, there is time for the tree to ripen the remaining buds to flower and crop the following year. So late-summer pruning is the best time if the tree does need pruning – if, for instance, it is over-crowded in the centre, or there are crossing branches. For the first couple of years or so, no pruning at all is desirable or required for bush or standard apples and pears.

How do you shock an eight-year-old 'Victoria' plum into bearing fruit? What should it be fed on and what can be done to prevent greenfly infestation which turns the leaves black?

PETER   Where 'Victoria' and other plum trees are growing too fast and too strongly, tie the young, six-month-old, longest branches over in a semi-circle to check the sap and encourage flower buds to form. This is called 'festooning'.

An alternative and even harsher treatment is to root-prune the tree. Here a semi-circular trench is dug, a foot (30 cm) or so deep, beneath and just within the outer spread of branches. All roots are severed. After root-pruning, the soil is replaced and the tree well staked. The next year the other half-circle is cut to check growth.

Usually the festooning is sufficient for young trees on semi-dwarfing rootstocks. For today's small gardens, the even more dwarfing and earlier fruiting Pixy rootstock is recommended for plums.

Plums flower quite early in the spring and the young developing fruitlets can be killed by late frost, so if the tree flowers satisfactorily but does not fruit, try to net some of the lower branches to give a little frost protection in spring.

Where the growth is excessive at the expense of fruit, either do not feed or just apply sulphate of potash in spring. Allow grass to grow beneath the tree as this will provide competition for plant food and water which encourages fruiting.

The black sooty mould that develops on the sweet honey-dew excreted by aphids is controlled by killing the aphids. A tar acid (tar oil) winter wash will kill overwintering aphid eggs, but you must beware because some plum and gage varieties can be damaged by this spray. Also, buds start to break early in mild springs and opening buds can be scorched by winter washes.

Spraying the young growths with pirimicarb kills the aphids and leaves their predators, such as ladybirds, unharmed. Where the tree is too tall to spray it all, use a systemic insecticide suitable for plums and cover as much foliage as you can. These insecticides are carried in the sap and give wider control. Always follow the manufacturer's instructions precisely when spraying.

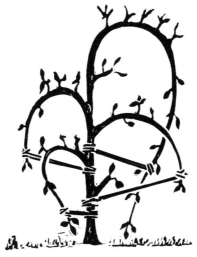

Festooning a plum tree

How do you identify an apple grown from a pip?

DAPHNE Unfortunately you can't, because apples do not come 'true' when grown from seed. When the tree finally bears fruit – and it is usually many years before it does when it is grown on its own roots – the fruit may resemble that of its 'mother' (the tree that bore the apple from which the pip was taken), its 'father' (the tree providing the pollen which fertilised the flower), or any one of the dozens of species making up the breeding lines of both of the parents, but it is unlikely to be exactly like the fruit you ate, or possibly any other apple in cultivation. The fruit may be quite palatable, or cook well, in which case it is worth growing on, but it is just as likely to be not particularly good. Unfortunately, you'll probably have some time to wait, and a large tree on your hands into the bargain, before you can find out.

New varieties of apple are usually the result of many years of research and specialised breeding programmes, although some of our favourites, especially older varieties, arose as chance seedlings. In the case of your tree, if you have plenty of space, I suggest you wait to see what kind of apples it produces and, if they are worth persevering with, you could then obtain some dwarfing rootstocks from a specialist fruit nursery and graft your apple onto these. The resulting trees will fruit earlier and remain a more manageable size, and the original can be disposed of, as it will probably be of a totally impracticable size by this time. On the other hand, you may feel all this is hardly worth the trouble, especially as it will need a compatible tree in the vicinity with which to pollinate it – if this isn't available you may not even get apples at all!

We are new allotment holders and have inherited some apple trees – both eaters and cookers. Could you give us advice on when to pick the fruit and how to store it? Last year we wrapped it in newspaper but all the eaters went soft and most of the cookers developed brown spots inside the flesh.

BILL   It is difficult for me to say when to pick the apples from the trees on this 'new' allotment you have, because I don't know whether they are early, mid-season or keeping varieties, and I don't doubt you are in the same boat. While all apples do not look alike, most apples look like apples. The appearance and condition of the fruit will have to be your guide, unless you can get someone skilful or lucky enough to identify the varieties. Many may be seedlings on their own roots and so be without a name.

But seeing that there are some eaters and cookers among these apples, you must sample them. If when trying to eat one your ears revolve, then that's a cooker, but whether it's a keeper-cooker further experience will be needed.

You start testing the apples that appear to be ready in late August. Those that eat well in August you can safely assume are early eaters, and then you delay the next test until early October, and some others may be ready then. A lot can be learned from how easily they part from the tree. You will find that the apples on the south side of the tree will be ripe before those on the north. And so you proceed through the months, until you get to the possibility of having some of the best-keeping desserts, such as 'Cox's Orange Pippin', 'Golden Delicious', 'Tydeman's Late Orange', or some of the best late cookers, such as 'Bramley's Seedling', 'Crawley Beauty', 'Howgate Wonder', 'Edward VII' or 'Newton Wonder'. There is no point in attempting to store early ripening dessert or cooking varieties – they just go woolly. So you only store late varieties, and they must be wrapped in waxed apple wraps – not newspaper, which tends to extract moisture from the fruit.

The apples must be stored cool and moist, and you should follow the old maxim that apples are stored in the cellar and pears in the attic.

I have been trying to grow strawberries in a barrel but so far haven't been very successful. Last year most of the fruit had a black mould on it. How can I get the kind of crop you see in advertisements?

DAPHNE   I don't think that the mould on your strawberries had anything to do with the fact that they were growing in a barrel. It was almost certainly caused by botrytis, a fungal disease which is worse in the kind of cold, wet summers we endured in 1986/87. The best method of control is to spray with a fungicide such as benomyl before the disease appears, and at 14-day intervals thereafter during the cropping season, removing any affected fruit as soon as you see it.

Having said that, I would be surprised if you'll ever achieve the kind of crop you see in advertisements, or even like the average crop you would get in the open ground, though I've had some very good yields from strawberries in growing bags. A lot depends on how you look after the barrel – it certainly won't look after itself. I find the best compost to fill the barrel is John Innes No. 2, but if you don't make your own it will be expensive to buy such a quantity, and the barrel will be very heavy, so you must pick the right spot first time. If you decide to use a peat-based compost, you will have to pay special attention to the feeding and watering. The barrel should be given a sheltered, sunny position. It should not be too close to a wall, as one side of it would be in permanent shade, unless yours is the kind with a rotating base.

A full-sized barrel will hold about 30 plants. Many varieties are suitable, but the newer ones like 'Rabunda', 'Totem' or the heavy cropping 'Cambridge Favourite' are particularly successful. It is easier to plant up the barrel as you fill it with compost, as the roots can be firmed in better.

During the growing and cropping season the compost must be kept uniformly moist. Purpose-designed barrels with a watering tube up the middle are easier to water evenly. As soon as the first flowers show, a tomato or other high-potash fertiliser should be given according to instructions. It is wise to net the ripening fruit to protect it from birds.

After three years both the plants and the compost should be replaced. Taking the cost of this and the original barrel into consideration, the growing of strawberries in this way is more of an 'impress your friends' exercise than a money-saving experiment.

A purpose-designed strawberry barrel with watering tube

My 'Cox's Orange Pippin' apple tree has little bits of 'cotton wool' on the branches. What is this and should I do anything about it?

PETER   The small pieces of cotton wool you aptly describe are the woolly, waxy protection excreted by woolly aphids. While small amounts will do little harm, where they build up in numbers, irregular swellings develop on twigs and branches. These swellings can split and allow entry of disease spores such as canker. Like all greenfly, greyfly, blackfly and other coloured aphids, they are better controlled in the early stages of attack.

This pest is quite easy to control once the insecticide has penetrated the waxy protection. Small patches are best controlled by applying malathion or HCH at spray strength with a brush in spring.

Where the attack is too widespread for spot treatment, the tree should be sprayed forcibly and thoroughly after flowering when the pest is active. Systemic insecticides such as dimethoate are likely to be more effective than contact insecticides like diluted HCH. The adult aphid overwinters under loose flakes of bark and it is not controlled by winter sprays of tar acid (tar oil).

Woolly aphid is not a native pest of the British Isles and it is thought to have been accidentally introduced into Britain from North America and was first noted in the 1780s. The American origins explain the old common name 'American blight'.

The British bred apple rootstocks called 'Malling Merton', such as 'MM106' and 'MM111', are resistant to woolly aphid and were bred in part to meet the needs of Australian fruit growers.

'Cox's Orange Pippin', although one of the best flavoured dessert apples and for this reason the most popular English apple, is temperamental and quite demanding to grow. It is best in the warmer South of England and in warm, sheltered gardens.

Trees of 'Cox' on dwarfing rootstocks such as 'Malling 9' will need secure staking for all their life and require a good soil to crop well. The recently introduced 'Malling 27' rootstock produces an even smaller tree but the root system is more secure than 'Malling 9' and recommended for this capricious pippin.

I have recently moved house and find I have a fruit garden containing raspberries, loganberries, blackberries, blackcurrants and gooseberries. I have no idea how to go about pruning these. I think they are about four years old.

BILL   I am assuming that you have moved house in February and found these soft fruits quite neglected. It is likely that the raspberries are summer-fruiting varieties and if there are many dark brown canes, which indicates they have fruited, and a lot of light brown canes, which will fruit in the current year, you should cut out the old, dark canes to their base. Then tie in the young canes to 14-gauge wires at a height of about 4 feet (122 cm).

Regarding blackberries and loganberries, cut out old, dark brown fruited wood, retain the lighter coloured canes and, if they are obviously out of hand, which they usually are, tip the growths back by a third.

Blackcurrants should have been pruned after the fruit was gathered the previous year. If they haven't, then remove now some central old canes, cutting them at their base, to produce a hollow, goblet-shaped bush. Retain the pale brown, younger canes.

Gooseberries are best pruned in spring, removing much of the central wood, so that air movement is freer and the fruit all that easier to gather.

Different pruning techniques are required for these soft fruits, depending on whether they are established or newly planted. To simplify matters, consider summer-fruiting raspberries. This is a perennial subject which produces canes of biennial life and then they are cut out. The loganberry and blackberry are very vigorous and two-year-old (or older) dark brown wood, which will have fruited, needs to be removed back to its base, so you are always encouraging new wood to be produced. The same applies to blackcurrants. The best crops are produced on one-year-old wood. It pays to cut out some of the old canes right to their base so that new growths are produced from soil level. Newly planted blackcurrants and raspberries should be cut back to within 4 inches (10 cm) of soil level, which means that they will not fruit until next year.

Heavily compost all soft fruit plants in spring, and hoe a handful or two of Growmore fertiliser around each. In all instances it is essential to control pests during spring and summer by frequent insecticide spraying after flowering.

Last year all the leaves of my gooseberry bushes were eaten by little caterpillars. This year the crop has been very poor and covered in grey mould. Can I do anything to get better results next year?

PETER   The gooseberry sawfly caterpillar attack may have weakened your gooseberry bushes and made them more prone to disease attack like mildew but other than this the two problems are unrelated.

Sawfly caterpillars can completely defoliate gooseberry bushes in a matter of days. If you see them at the first signs of attack it is fairly easy to pick them off. Spraying offers a sure and more complete control. Any good caterpillar killer, such as resmethrin, fenitrothion or derris, sprayed at the first sign of attack, will kill them.

Remember, the adult emerges from April onwards and the life cycle from egg to caterpillar and then adult again is eight weeks. Some three generations are possible in a year so keep an eye out for signs of eaten leaves throughout late spring and summer.

Grey-to-white felty moulds on fruits and leaves is caused by the disease American gooseberry mildew. As the attack intensifies the grey turns felty brown and the disease can spread to red, black and other members of the *Ribes* (currant) family. Mildew can be wiped off infected fruits which will then be quite all right to eat.

Careful pruning to allow free movement of air through the branches and the removal of diseased tips of branches will help to reduce attack. Avoid planting in damp, shaded places, keep weeds beneath the plant under control and do not feed excessively with high nitrogen fertilisers. Even with these cultural treatments it will be necessary to spray with a systemic fungicide, such as bupirimate and triforine, to keep the leaves and fruits clean.

New cultivars, such as the gooseberry 'Invicta' and the black currant 'Ben More', are immune to infection and much heavier yielding than older kinds.

All the leaves on my fan-trained 'Peregrine' peach tree turn red and blistered and eventually drop off. Is this harmful to the tree?

BILL   It is obvious that the peach is attacked by a very common disease of the family, called *Taphrina deformans*, commonly known as peach leaf curl. This disease does not only ruin peaches; it is common among other members of the *Prunus* family, like almonds, nectarines and apricots. In the past the most effective control was to spray with lime-sulphur wash, but this is no longer available.

Once you see the thickened, reddish-purple, puckered leaves it is almost too late to do anything, so preventive spraying is indicated. Winter-wash in late December or early January with tar acid. Spray with mancozeb or liquid copper fungicide in late February. Repeat 14 days later and just before petal fall. A thorough drenching of all the branches and twigs is necessary. If pests are also present, mix the fungicide with an appropriate pesticide. Use a broad spectrum insecticide, e.g. permethrin, or, if aphids only are present, use a specific aphicide, e.g. pirimicarb.

Another spraying that is necessary, to control overwintering pests, is to drench very thoroughly in late December, and only then, with tar acid wash. If there are green plants or bulbs emerging under the trees, then cover them with two or three sheets of newspaper before spraying. Spraying should only be carried out on a calm, non-frosty day.

An important and obvious part of garden hygiene is to collect any infected leaves and burn them. This burning of 'green' material has always been the gardener's solution and it was easy enough when the garden bonfire was part of the fun of the thing. But now it is considered unhealthy and anti-social, so you have to get rid of these leaves, and also any rose foliage infected with black spot, by burying 2 feet (61 cm) deep.

What is big-bud on blackcurrants and what can be done about it?

DAPHNE   'Big-bud' is a condition caused by the blackcurrant gall mite, and can also sometimes affect gooseberries and red currants. The tiny pests are carried by the wind or on other insects in spring and early summer. They enter the buds and feed and breed inside them, causing the characteristically round, swollen buds so unlike the pointed healthy ones. The following spring they leave the withering, mutilated buds and transfer to the newly forming ones. Apart from weakening the bushes and affecting cropping, the blackcurrant gall mite transmits *reversion*, a serious virus disease which reduces cropping severely and for which there is no cure.

Reversion can be difficult to identify, but usually appears as a change in leaf shape. The main lobe has less than five main veins and there is no basal cleft. Also the normally grey flower buds have a red tinge. Bushes showing signs of reversion should be removed and burnt. However in an increasing number of areas garden fires are now banned by byelaws, in which case the only means of disposal is the local authority refuse tip. Garden fires are the cause of much controversy at present.

Blackcurrant bushes should be regularly checked for the first signs of big-bud, then affected buds can be picked off immediately and burnt. It has been found that spraying with benomyl when the first flowers open and twice afterwards at 14-day intervals has some control over the mite. Badly infested bushes should be disposed of as they are almost certain to be affected by reversion.

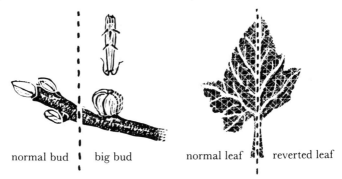

normal bud   big bud   normal leaf   reverted leaf

'Big bud' and reversion in blackcurrant bushes

I have tried for several years to grow good leeks but three-quarters of them always go to seed. All the allotments round mine seem to have the same problem.

PETER   There are two kinds of leek. The most commonly grown is the long, blanch-shafted type; well-known varieties include 'Lyon' and 'Musselburgh'. Then there are the so-called pot leeks, popular in the North-East of England where they are often grown for showing; these are much thicker and squatter in shape.

The long types are raised from seed sown in March and the seedlings are planted out several inches deep in early summer. Pot leeks are grown from 'pips', or small plantlets. These are produced by shearing over the flower head before the flowers set seeds. Small plantlets then develop at the base of the short, thin flower stems.

These pips are then potted up and grown under glass through the winter ready to plant up in spring.

Both seedlings and plantlets have the flower head triggered by a check to growth in their early stages of life. Where they have been started into rapid growth early in the year in the warm and then subjected to some cold night temperatures, this has the same effect as winter conditions on full-sized leeks. This is one explanation for early seed head production.

Some cultivars and strains of pot leeks are not as good as others and one possible weakness is the tendency towards premature flowering.

All leeks need fertile soil to grow well. Dig in lots of well-rotted manure or garden compost in the autumn. Then allow the soil to settle well before spring planting. While the organic matter will help to retain moisture, they will need plenty of water during their period of rapid growth in summer and early autumn.

On light, sandy soils lack of water can cause a check to growth and this can also prompt premature flowering. If the soil is quick-drying this could account for neighbouring plots having a similar problem.

I would like some advice on the harvesting and storing of onions, as mine usually develop neck rot.

GEOFFREY Rotting in store can be a result of the onion bulbs not being fully ripe.

Do not bend the leaves over at the neck as an aid to ripening. This merely renders the bulbs vulnerable to rot. Just let the leaves yellow and fall over naturally. Check growth and so encourage thorough ripening by going along the rows with a fork and just lifting the bulbs enough to break the roots. When the roots and skin are thoroughly dry, store in a cool, dry, frost-free building.

Bulbs that are apparently fully ripe and free from disease or soft rots when placed in store and which then decay are probably infected with a fungus disease called neck rot. The bulbs soften and then infection shows as a grey mould around the top or neck. Because the disease is carried on the onion seed, control is not difficult. I just shake the seed up in a fungicide dust before sowing them. Onion sets can be treated by soaking them in a solution of the same material. Benomyl is the chemical most often recommended as a control for neck rot.

Clean up every scrap of debris left from the previous onion crop and get rid of it by composting. Use this compost in the ornamental garden.

Every year my French beans have a disease which causes the leaves to turn brown and finally the plants collapse. Some years my peas are similarly affected. I have been told there is a foot rot organism in the soil and the cure is to sterilise it with formaldehyde. Is there any alternative?

BILL   A frequent disease of French beans is anthracnose, and the seeds are sometimes attacked by bean beetle, which is very destructive indeed. Your plants collapse following germination, and this does suggest the fungus disease anthracnose. The symptoms are black spots which extend to circular or oval pits edged with red. The disease also penetrates the pods and infects the seeds.

Most sources of commercially saved seeds are free of this disease, but if you have saved your own seeds from infected stock then that is the reason the trouble is being perpetuated. It is possibly being exacerbated by too damp soil conditions, conceivably allied to excessive shade.

So the controls are to treat the seeds before sowing with a benomyl seed dressing, after making as sure as you can that the seeds are 'clean' anyway. The position where you grow the beans must be well drained, with rich soil and in full sun. A handful of superphosphate of lime per yard (m) run is indicated because beans have a high phosphate requirement, especially early in their life. As soon as the seedlings are about 2 inches (5 cm) high, spray them with mancozeb or liquid copper fungicide, and spray the plants again after flowering.

Some of your peas are similarly affected in that they collapse following germination. Again a seed dressing is indicated, although many firms do treat pea seeds with a fungicidal dressing when they are packed. Spraying with liquid copper fungicide when the seedlings are around 2 inches (5 cm) high is essential.

You suggest sterilising the soil with formaldehyde. This chemical has no clearance for amateur gardener use. I would recommend tar acid as an alternative.

I bought two packets of marrow seeds, one trailing and one bush. About 75 per cent of the seeds turned out to be male. Can seed companies tell when packing the seeds which are male and which are female?

GEOFFREY Fortunately for the general well being of marrows and the sanity of gardeners, male and female flowers grow on the same plant.

In dull, cool weather there often seems to be a surplus of 'one sex' flowers. To try and offset this I keep two or three non-cropping plants growing on in small pots to get them rootbound. This way I am sure of a constant supply of male flowers. Stripping the surplus male flowers from the cropping plants, I hope, will stimulate them into producing female flowers. These are then pollinated using a male flower from the potbound plants.

Keeping the soil well watered, sheltering young plants from cold winds and spraying the leaves over in dry weather should be routine marrow-growing practice. When plants reach cropping size, watering with a high potash liquid feed often proves effective.

a: Female flower   b: Male flower
Hand-pollination is only necessary in dull or cold weather when there are no insects about

How do you stop cauliflowers from 'bolting'?

GEOFFREY The obvious and facetious answer is – lock the garden gate.

One of the unfortunate consequences of growing cauliflowers from F_1 seed is that the curds all reach maturity at the same time. I would try one of the non-F_1 types. 'All the Year Round' is an old favourite which is suitable for successional sowing.

In dry weather, keep the soil well watered and shade mature curds from direct sunlight. The golden rules for the would-be cauliflower grower are as follows. First prepare the soil by working in well-rotted organic matter – deep and rich is the maxim. Secondly, during the whole of the growing period there must be no check to growth, so be careful when transplanting and water regularly. Finally, buy a deep-freeze to preserve surplus heads.

The foliage of my carrots is stunted and yellowish-brown. The carrots are only 2 inches (5 cm) long and some of them have small white maggots in them. What can be done?

DAPHNE   The small white maggots are almost certainly the larvae of the carrot fly. The leaves turn reddish and wilt, seedlings will be killed and mature roots are tunnelled and eventually rot. The carrot fly is attracted to the carrots by the smell, so it is important not to handle the tops any more than possible. The seed should be sown thinly and any thinning out of young plants should be done on a cool, dull, still day to reduce the smell emitted by the bruised leaves; thinnings should be removed immediately. Carrot fly is worst in dry, sandy soils so adequate watering will help.

There is no cure for the damaged roots but there are preventative measures that can be taken. Use a soil insecticide such as bromophos at sowing time and dust with insecticide at the soil surface as the roots develop. Some people claim that sowing rows of carrots alternately with a strong-smelling crop like onions will help to mask the carrot smell. Lifting early varieties before August and sowing maincrop varieties in June will have some benefit as these times miss the successive generations of the fly. Watering with an insecticide will also control this pest.

If the roots are hollowed rather than tunnelled, and the grubs are larger, these are probably larvae of the swift moth. Control is difficult, but picking out and destroying the caterpillars and using a soil insecticide are the best methods.

Sometimes discoloured foliage can have another cause, especially if there isn't root damage. The carrot-willow aphid is the most likely culprit, producing distorted leaves and stunted roots. This insect can also transmit the motley dwarf virus, which shows itself as a yellow mottling of the centre leaves with a reddish colouring of the older ones. The crop will be seriously affected, and so it is essential that the carrot-willow aphid is controlled by spraying with an insecticide such as pyrethrum, pirimicarb or permethrin as soon as infestation is noticed.

These pests and diseases will also affect other members of the carrot family, like parsnips and parsley, and also related wild species, so it is wise to keep the weed population down in the vegetable garden.

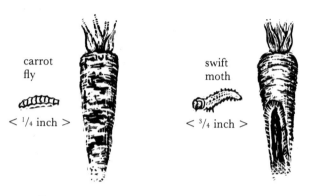

The carrot fly tunnels through the root; the swift moth hollows it out

I sowed 'Citadel' sprouts at the end of January and planted them out at the end of May. They have all gone to seed. Why has this happened?

PETER   Sowing too early is the most likely explanation for your sprouts running to seed. 'Citadel' is a good F_1 hybrid, bred for harvesting from December to March, in other words one of the later-maturing cultivars.

It is possible to sow sprouts in January and produce monster plants with very high yields but if you do this the seedlings and plants have to be kept growing with no check to growth, especially from low temperatures in early spring.

Just delay the sowing to March and early April and you will have no further trouble. We tend to overlook the remarkable advances made in plant breeding in recent years. Thirty years ago Brussels sprouts were all cross-pollinated and open seeding, with considerable variation from plant to plant down the row. Some plants had good stems of fairly tight sprouts while others were all open and leafy.

Breeding F_1 hybrids has changed all that and now plants are carefully pollinated to produce remarkably uniform and heavy-cropping plants. A selection of F_1 hybrid cultivars is needed to crop through the season. For example, 'Peer Gynt' for October to December, 'Widgeon' for November to February, 'Citadel' and 'Fortress' for December to March.

These cropping periods are for the main weight of crop and in average garden conditions the harvest period can be much longer than the months listed. 'Peer Gynt', for example, will still be producing some sprouts in February. Where the stems are left with a few tiny sprouts at the top they will sprout to produce several pickings of succulent young shoots. Cooked as spring greens they make a tasty spring vegetable.

The young tops can also be cut from sprouts to eat as greens. Picking these in late autumn can help the development of sprouts lower down the stem. Do not, however, take the tops out too early. 'Ormavon' is a garden sprout which produces a small cabbage on the top of each stem of good sprouts.

The blossom on my kidney beans drops off before it sets. What can I do to prevent this?

BILL   Your kidney beans are subject to blossom drop, and I presume you are referring to runner beans, because French beans are seldom so troubled because their flowers are self-fertile. On the other hand, the flower of the runner bean is self-sterile and depends entirely on the visitation of a bee or other pollinating insect on the very day the flower opens. By careful scrutiny of the runner bean flower during summer you can tell whether that flower has been visited by a bee and so naturally pollinated. It is possible to spot the bee's 'footprint' on the flower, and when that is seen it is long odds that the flower will 'pod up'.

Runner beans frequently do not crop well in the early part of the summer, even though they may have flowered well, and this is nearly always due to bees and other pollinating insects being scarce because of cool or windy weather. Later in the season, towards August/September, beans always set well and produce satisfactory crops.

There are other causes of bud and flower drop in runner beans. One is poor root action. It is essential to grow runner beans in a sunny position; the soil must be very rich, deeply dug and well drained. The runner bean has a high phosphate requirement, so apply superphosphate of lime or basic slag at a couple of handfuls per yard (m) run of trench before covering with soil.

In cold districts it is wise to germinate runner beans in peat pots or soil blocks in a greenhouse or garden frame, so that a good young plant can be put out in its cropping position the first week or so in June.

◇

My beetroot seedlings are about 4 inches (10 cm) high but all the leaves are yellow and withered and the tips are dying. Is this a disease, or could it be wind scorch as they are in a very exposed position?

DAPHNE   I don't think wind can be the cause of this problem. Although the seeds are sometimes slow to germinate, beetroot is usually a trouble-free crop if it is given a sunny site with a neutral or slightly alkaline soil, and liberal watering in dry spells to prevent woodiness.

The condition you describe sounds like 'speckled yellows'. The leaf between the veins starts to turn yellow; if the condition is very bad the whole leaf turns yellow and brown and withers with the edges rolling inwards. 'Speckled yellows' is caused by a lack of manganese in the soil and usually occurs in a highly alkaline soil or one that has been overlimed. Avoid adding lime to the part of the garden in which you grow beetroot unless you know the soil is acid, and use a fertiliser containing 'chelated' trace elements. Watering with a sequestrene compound containing manganese, or a 'plant tonic' will correct the condition if it hasn't gone too far.

Browning on leaves can sometimes be caused by mangold fly, or leaf miner, the grubs of which tunnel inside the leaves, causing blisters which eventually turn brown. The best method of control is to pick off and destroy affected leaves. I don't think this is the trouble in your case because of the yellow colour you describe. Nor do I think it is the other cause of seedlings shrivelling and dying – black leg – which occurs if the seed is sown too thickly or the soil is waterlogged; it can be controlled to a certain extent by watering with Cheshunt Compound.

I have just dug up my potatoes and they are ruined by slugs. I put slug pellets in when planting. Can you suggest anything else I could try next year? Slugs are a problem in general in my garden.

GEOFFREY Unfortunately, slugs thrive under the very conditions which gardeners provide when trying to improve soil fertility. A deep, well worked, humus-rich soil offers a slug equivalent of a four star hotel and under these conditions it is impossible to eliminate them completely. The best that can be hoped for is to reduce the damage done to an acceptable level.

Do not leave heaps of rotting vegetation lying about on the garden for slugs to shelter and breed under. The compost heap is the best place for all plant debris.

Improve surface drainage by bastard trenching (breaking up the subsoil with a fork during the routine winter cultivations). Prior to planting, set up the potato plot in the old-fashioned ridges. This is one of the best controls for slugs in my experience, particularly on heavy land.

Grow only first and second earlies which are off the land fairly quickly. Main crop left on cold wet soil until late autumn are particularly vulnerable to soil pests.

Try planting a row or two under black polythene. The soil is prepared in the usual way; then the tubers are spaced out and then just covered by a handful of moist peat. The polythene is laid down the rows and anchored firmly either with soil or bricks. As the potatoes grow, cut slits to let them through the polythene cover into the light. Tubers form on the soil surface under the polythene cover. Slug pellets placed under the polythene will be lethal only to gastropods, not to birds, toads, hedgehogs and so on.

Planting potatoes in ridges

Planting potatoes under black polythene

In July my potato tops turned yellow and shed their leaves. Then the stems started rotting from the top downwards. I got a reasonable crop when I dug them up but I want to know what caused the death of the plants and if the tubers are safe to eat.

PETER   Premature yellowing and leaf fall are symptoms of the fungus disease potato blight. Usually the first signs of attack are brown and black spots on the leaves, often worse on the leaf edges and tips of shoots.

This disease spreads rapidly in warm, damp weather and in wet summers it spreads very quickly through crops to do immense damage. It was the series of blight epidemics in the 1840s that caused the Irish potato famine.

Tubers from infected tops can be quite all right and perfectly edible. Disease spores will, however, wash down from the foliage and infect the tubers. Here they form brown spots which spread to infect the whole tuber and make it inedible. Often secondary disease infection also attacks the diseased tubers and causes wet, evil-smelling rots in damp conditions.

The disease is carried over from one year to the next on diseased tubers, so clear the land after each crop and prevent old potatoes growing on compost heaps. Even so, in bad blight years the disease is likely to spread in the wind over considerable distances.

Where this disease is a regular problem, you should apply a protective spray based on zineb (Dithane) in early July and then at fortnightly intervals. If you have just an occasional case, cut off the foliage at the first signs of attack and lift early to prevent tuber damage.

Because this disease does not really get a hold until mid-summer, early cultivars are usually lifted before it becomes a problem. Good early-maturing kinds are 'Maris Bard' and 'Home Guard'.

This disease also infects *outdoor* tomatoes and causes dark spots on the green fruits; mature fruits rot very quickly and are inedible. Spray or dust tomatoes every 10 days or so from the time the first small fruits appear. The dry atmosphere under glass usually prevents this disease attacking greenhouse tomatoes.

I want to make really good compost. What is the best size and shape to make the heap? Are activators worth while? And are there certain things I should not add, e.g. privet clippings, rhubarb leaves, grass cuttings and weeds, especially those that have been treated with weedkillers?

DAPHNE   Compost is the substance which is produced when vegetable waste rots down, mainly through bacterial activity. What results should be crumbly, good as a humus-rich soil conditioner and contain some plant nutrients.

The larger the heap the better because, while rotting, a large proportion of it should heat up sufficiently to destroy weed seeds and roots, and pests and fungal diseases. I find that if space allows, two heaps side by side are useful, as you can be taking compost off one while stocking the other. Enclosing the sides with timber or corrugated iron sheeting will keep the heap tidy and it will warm up better. Excess rain should be excluded by covering the top with ventilated polythene or something similar. The uncomposted material at the top of the heap can be used as a basis for a new one.

Most vegetable waste can be composted, but very woody material will rot down slowly so it should be shredded first. Even newspaper will rot in time. The main thing is to use a variety of textures, well mixed. Thick layers of grass mowings will turn into a disgusting green mess if some air is not admitted by mixing them with coarser

A compost heap, showing alternate layers of fine and coarse waste

material to encourage the right sort of bacteria. Too much coarse waste will have too much air in it to heat up and rot properly, so it should be mixed with some finer rubbish. There is no reason why you should not use moderate quantities of the kind of garden waste you list, provided they are mixed with other things, but autumn leaves should be placed in a heap on their own to form leaf-mould, as they rot down very slowly, usually by fungal rather than by bacterial action.

Whether you put weeds treated with herbicides on the heap will largely depend on the chemical used. Weedol and Tumbleweed are deactivated on contact with the soil and organic matter, making any residue harmless to plants. Selective lawn weedkillers will usually say on the label how long the composting time should be and is usually six months or longer. Some plants, like tomatoes and sweet peas, are very sensitive to such chemicals, however, so compost known to contain treated weeds should be kept away.

A correctly made heap should rot down without the use of activators, though they certainly speed up the process. They usually contain lime, which prevents the compost becoming too acid, and nitrogen. It is not necessary to add layers of soil – there are enough bacteria on the roots of the waste material and soil can actually slow down the process by cooling the heap off. Similarly, a good heap should not need watering – there should be enough moisture in the rubbish, providing a good variety of material is used.

I have taken over an allotment which is overrun with twitch, bindweed and horsetail. Is there a weedkiller which will deal with these, which is safe for children and pets?

GEOFFREY Horsetail is so deep rooted that forking and hand-weeding it out is a problem. You could spend 12 months as I did 10 years ago forking and hand-weeding. This will reduce the weed population enough to get the land into crop. Routine cultivations – digging, hoeing, and mulching – will complete the cleaning process.

The next occasion a similar problem presented itself, this time a weed-infested raspberry bed, I used a total weedkiller. Once the raspberry canes were out, sodium chlorate put down in September (not forgetting to treat the paths as well) left weed-free ground for sowing seed into during April the following year. I did, of course, dig the soil over in the normal way during February to make sure all the chemical had leached out.

On bindweed and couch grass you could use one of the modern weed controls based on the chemical glyphosate. Do the spraying when the weeds have a good leaf cover and repeat on any surviving or new growth at four-week intervals until cleared. The chemical is not held in the soil and you could be sowing seed almost immediately. Remember that when using chemicals you need full protective clothing to avoid irritation to eyes and skin.

Horsetail is not easily controlled with glyphosate. The most effective treatment is dichlobenil (Casoron G4). This does mean that replanting cannot take place for 12 months. Sodium chlorate, although less thorough, would be a better option where the problem is not too well established.

Mulching with black polythene I discovered to be one step in advance of useless.

What causes club root in cabbages, can it spread, and what harm does it do to the ground? Can other plants, such as dahlias and chrysanthemums, be grown in infected soil?

PETER   Club root only attacks plants grouped under the name *Cruciferae*, that is, all the green cabbage-like vegetables including cauliflower, Brussels sprouts, broccoli, calabrese, savoys, kales, etc. and such root vegetables as turnip, kohl rabi, radish and swede. It is worth remembering that the swede 'Marian' is resistant to this disease and to mildew. There are flowers, too, in the *Cruciferae* family, and so stocks, wallflower and candytuft are likely to be attacked where the soil is infected.

The first signs of attack are wilting on hot days and plant recovery overnight. When lifted the plant roots are swollen and distorted, either in one big lump – hence the common name club root – or a cluster of swollen roots rather like dahlia tubers, which prompt the other common name 'finger-and-toe disease'. Advanced stages of attack will produce a soft, evil-smelling wet rot.

Be aware of similar root swellings on these plants after attack by cabbage root fly maggots. You can identify the presence of this pest by cutting through the swelling. In this case it will be hollow, tunnelled and in some cases the maggot or larvae will be seen.

There is no tunnelling with club root which can survive as resting spores in the soil, even in the absence of host plants, for over 20 years. This disease is much worse in acid and waterlogged land. You can add lime to take the pH reading – what we call the acid/alkaline level of soils – well above 7. However, the alkaline conditions will suit greens but not potatoes which can suffer a severe scab attack in such soil.

Earthing up diseased plants encourages new roots to form and helps to get a crop. Dig out and destroy diseased roots after cropping. Growing young plants in disease-free potting soil and treating plant roots with systemic fungicide dips also reduces the damage.

Where greens have to be grown in infected land, if each plant is set out in a double handful of disease-free soil, acceptable crops can be grown.

How do you prevent cabbage white butterflies from laying their eggs on brassicas, and the subsequent devouring of the plants by the caterpillars?

GEOFFREY Several years ago I had two Siamese cats who spent hours in the garden butterfly hunting. They kept the brassicas caterpillar-free. The problem is cats cannot be guaranteed or for that matter trained to do that. I would suggest netting the crop with the white film that is normally used to protect growing plants from frost. This will prove an effective barrier against egg-laying butterflies.

Spraying once the caterpillars hatch with a bacterium (*Bacillus thuringiensis*) which stops them feeding and, consequently, starving them to death is an ultra-modern pest control. You need to hit every caterpillar directly for this to be fully effective. Or spray with derris, an old-fashioned way admittedly, yet safe and effective if you apply it frequently enough. A modern spray, permethrin, would be equally safe, even more effective and requires less frequent use.

Simply removing the caterpillars and dropping them into salt water is my own safe, simple and effective way, which offers no risk to anything other than cabbage white butterflies.

◇

What causes the hearts of celery to turn brown and rot?

BILL   There are a few different causes of celery heart rot. The trouble can be to do with varieties and it is a fact that many of the trench varieties, such as 'Giant Pink' or 'Giant Red' or 'Solid White', are prone to this trouble. Possibly this is because they are blanched by the exclusion of light and if the blanching process is too early then the heart does not respond, does not make further growth and rots away. This trouble will be more likely if the soil in the trench is short of phosphates, and a basic slag or superphosphate of lime dressing earlier would be indicated.

Another possibility is that there may be a boron deficiency in the soil. Normally this is a minor element, but in celery cultivation it takes on the importance of a major element. To make sure there is no such boron deficiency you should spray the seedlings when they are in the frame or box, before planting out, with a liquid fertiliser that contains boron. And when the plants are put outdoors and are about 4 to 5 inches (10 to 13 cm) high, drench again with this liquid fertiliser.

Self-blanching varieties of celery are now being grown more and more, because of ease of cultivation, and modern varieties like 'Ivory Tower', 'Golden Self-Blanching' and 'American Green', are of good quality. Nevertheless, self-blanching varieties are just as prone to heart rot as trench varieties and all the earlier suggestions for control apply, plus frequent use of slug pellets.

UNDER GLASS

GREENHOUSES OFTEN SEEM TO BE STATUS SYMBOLS
to me. If you have a greenhouse it probably means not only that
your home is better equipped than most, but also that you know a
thing or two about gardening. Of course the fact is that these days
millions of ordinary homes boast greenhouses of every shape and
size. Owning one no longer brings status, unless it's large enough for
the estate agent to call a 'conservatory'. (Actually that's a bad
example because, let's face it, an estate agent will call a glazed porch
a conservatory.) However, I still feel that having a greenhouse in the
garden somehow implies you are that bit cleverer when it comes to
matters horticultural. Your fingers are perhaps a shade or two
greener. You don't just mow the lawn and cut the hedge, you also
put things in pots, take cuttings and generally *nurture* in a way which
leaves others far behind.

Actually, *I* happen to have a greenhouse, and I find it extremely
useful. The mower goes in there, as do various buckets and brooms –
not to mention the bike. It's just a transparent garden shed, I
suppose, which is no doubt a terrible waste of a facility. The
wretched thing was there when we bought the house. Some day I
must get round to planting things in pots and justify its existence.

JOHN THIRLWELL

I have raised 15 kiwi fruit plants which are now 8 inches (20 cm) high. How do I distinguish males from females? At the moment they are in a cold greenhouse. What temperatures do they need and can you advise on the positioning of the plants?

GEOFFREY Until the young kiwi fruit plants grow to maturity and then flower, sexing them could prove difficult. When your seedlings do flower, check the individual cream-coloured florets with a hand lens. Male flowers will carry stamens only. The female flowers have a stigma, style and ovary which is a small swelling at the base of the petals.

There are kiwi fruits which are hermaphrodite (male and female parts in one flower). I know of one such in Derby, growing on a south-facing fence, and it fruits well.

Plant selected seedlings in a deep, humus-rich soil and in a south-facing position. The root system is shallow, so keep the soil mulched and well supplied with water. The shoots will need support, and as the crop is produced on the current season's shoots you should prune regularly. You may have to hand-pollinate. Kiwi fruit (*Actinidia deliciosa*) will soon outgrow the average size of greenhouse.

What is the best way to plant and prune a fig tree under glass, and what is the best variety for this type of cultivation?

BILL   There are not many fruits with the delicious flavour and quality of a fresh fig, which in warm climates may well produce three crops of fruit a year. But in this country the only fruit likely to appear and mature is borne on the previous year's shoots. In our climate the fig outdoors grows very freely, almost too freely, and some restriction of the root growth by stones or slates is indicated.

On the other hand, the best variety for British gardens, whether indoors or out, which is 'Brown Turkey', will have a better chance of cropping satisfactorily if grown in a cold greenhouse, ideally a lean-to, with the fig planted against a south-facing wall. The soil should be rich loam with some manure and a little John Innes Base Fertiliser (this contains a mix of superphosphate, hoof and horn and sulphate of potash, and is obtainable from some garden centres and shops). There should be root restriction, so that the fig doesn't 'go mad'.

Pruning is carried out in early July when excessive shoots are thinned out, and again in April when unripened shoots are removed and the ones from the previous year carrying the flower buds are tied in.

So the basics of fig cultivation are choice of variety, a not too rich soil, full sun, a certain amount of root restriction, judicious pruning and the recognition that figs must always be ripened on the tree. If picked too young they are woolly and tasteless, and that is why in our country they are best grown under glass.

The fig has a rather unusual flower arrangement in that it has a hollow vessel enclosing numerous flowers which never see the light yet develop and ripen their seeds. There are, of course, other subjects of which we eat the undeveloped flowers, such as globe artichokes and cauliflowers.

I intend to buy a greenhouse and as I have never owned one before I would appreciate practical advice on where to site it in my garden, how to run it and the best kind of heater to use.

BILL   If you have the space it is a must to have a greenhouse because then your interest in gardening can be year-round. If you have no greenhouse and no frame, then you are not enjoying gardening in its totality – the sowing of seeds, the taking of cuttings, the growing on of a plant, be it vegetable, fruit or flower, from its early stages to maturity.

The type of greenhouse really depends on your keenness and the depth of your pocket. If money is no object, choose a glass greenhouse with a structure of aluminium alloy or cedar-wood. There are many cheaper greenhouses, some of rather flimsy construction covered with polythene, which has a limited life.

The orientation of a greenhouse depends much on the layout of your garden and the position of the house, the garage and any trees. There is little point in positioning a greenhouse under trees. If they are deciduous trees then the greenhouse will get reasonable light in winter but unsatisfactory light in summer. If the trees are evergreen and on the south or the west side, then there would be very poor light summer, autumn and winter. If the aim is primarily autumn and winter cultivation, the greenhouse should run east to west. If the aim is mainly spring and summer growing, then it should run north to south. But these are the ideals. What is necessary is maximum natural light, with some shelter from the north and the east to reduce heat loss.

The best method of heating is by thermostatically controlled electric fan. If this is not possible then the next best is by gas or by solid fuel heating circulating water. If this is not on then paraffin, natural gas or bottled gas can be used to heat either air or water. If any of these last three are used, constant ventilation is essential because of build-up of toxic gases and considerable increase in atmospheric humidity.

I am going on holiday for three weeks in September. What is the best way of keeping all the plants happy in my lean-to greenhouse which has automatic-opening vents?

PETER   Three weeks is quite a long time and the weather can be hot in September. While most plants will be all right unattended for this period if well fed and clear of pests and diseases on departure, arrangements will be necessary to keep the plants adequately watered.

Most greenhouses are heavily shaded at this time and, even with automatic ventilation, painting the glass with white shading material to reduce the temperature within the house and to cut down water loss will be very important. There are a number of capillary watering systems, both proprietary and home-made, which will maintain a supply of water to plants in pots and growing bags.

It is essential to have these watering systems up and working well for several weeks before you go away. Then any faults can be corrected and the amount of water needed can be assessed.

The first and most important thing to remember is that water will travel up a wick or capillary mat for $2^{1}/_{2}$ inches (6 cm). Once the water level in any reservoir drops below this it will not move upwards. This usually means having a wide rather than a deep volume of water for the wicks to pull from.

Capillary watering systems for pots and growing bags

For capillary mats to work, the container-grown or potted plants will need to be stood on the mat and watered well from above. This water then runs right through the compost – moistening it on the way – and makes contact with the mat. Then the capillary line of water movement is set up. As moisture dries from the compost, more is drawn up from the mat (or wick in the case of wicks).

Should a pot be lifted and the contact broken, it may prove necessary to water the plant well from above to set the capillary action off again. Some dilute liquid feed can of course be included to feed as well as water while you are away.

My aubergine plants never start setting fruit before it's time to clean the greenhouse out for the winter. Any tips on getting the flowers to set earlier?

PETER   Aubergines are quite slow-growing in their early stages and although they need cultural conditions very similar to tomatoes it is advisable to sow them at least a month earlier. For most gardeners the best protection that can be provided is a cold greenhouse and this means putting the young plants into the house in May. Put them out earlier and they are likely to be checked, if not killed, by low night temperatures.

Even if you have no greenhouse they can be grown in warm and sheltered gardens but here the planting is late May under cloches and early June outside.

Early sowing, however, is critical for all these plantings and quite large plants in 5¹/₂ inches (14 cm) pots need to be grown first in heat. While there is some competition for window-sill space in March and April, this is by far the best place for home gardeners to raise aubergines. Given this luxury they can be sown in February and good sized flowering plants will then be achieved by planting time.

Don't grow too many if space indoors is limited; three well grown plants will produce a heavy crop. Spray them regularly to control greenfly and whitefly – these pests like aubergines quite as much as we do!

The one tip I have found useful is to remove the dying petals as the tiny purple – or white – fruits begin to develop. Left in place the old petals rot and this rot can spread back to the fruits, especially in cold, damp conditions.

This plant is quite attractive, with deep purple stems, dark leaves and bright yellow and purple flowers. It makes a very attractive patio plant but, once again, buy a large plant to start with or sow indoors early in the year.

I have recently bought three sweet pepper plants and intend growing them in pots in my unheated greenhouse. I have never grown sweet peppers before and would like some advice.

DAPHNE   Sweet peppers (capsicums) need similar growing conditions to tomatoes, to which they are related. Your plants will have been raised under heated glass and therefore will not be ready for planting in your unheated greenhouse until May, when the weather has warmed up somewhat. I have had great success with peppers planted three to a growing bag, but 9 inch pots (23 cm) filled with good quality peat-based compost can be used instead. If you are using pots rather than growing bags the plants should be potted-on into progressively larger ones until the final size is reached, rather than over-potting them immediately into 9 inch (23 cm) ones.

The plants should be watered regularly, but not over-watered. Once the first fruits have begun to form a tomato feed should be added to the water. Mature plants can reach 3 feet (91 cm) or more in height, and should be supported by tying to wires or canes. You'll have to keep a look-out for the two main pests of sweet peppers – aphids and red spider mite. Thorough spraying with permethrin should help to control aphids. Red spider mite is worse in very dry air conditions and so misting the plants with water will help the problem and also improve fruit set. Use a systemic insecticide such as pirimiphos-methyl or dimethoate two or three times until the pest is eradicated.

The peppers can be picked as soon as they are large enough for culinary purposes. Green peppers left on the plant to ripen will eventually turn red but waiting for this considerably reduces the weight of the final crop.

How do you get rid of whitefly from the greenhouse? I have tried all the sprays and fumigants without success.

PETER   Once you have the small pest whitefly in a greenhouse it is very difficult, if not impossible, to get rid of completely. The adult overwinters in nooks and crannies so a very thorough wash-down of the glass and glazing bars with garden disinfectant each autumn certainly helps to control them.

They hibernate in cold weather and then breed rapidly once the temperature rises in summer. Where a greenhouse is heated to 15°C (60°F) year-round, then this pest is a year-round problem. When you brush infested plant leaves the adult flies take to the wing and with heavy attacks virtually fill the air.

Each adult lays up to 200 eggs beneath the leaves of plants and in 8 to 10 days young nymphs hatch and form immobile scales. After feeding for two weeks they pupate and, in a temperature of 20°C (70°F), the period from egg to adult takes three weeks. It takes four weeks at 15°C (60°F) and much longer at lower temperatures.

Most contact insecticides, such as those based on resmethrin, permethrin and malathion, kill the adults, but larvae are more difficult to kill and so repeated sprays at three-to-four-day intervals for three weeks will be needed to kill all stages. Some control can also be gained by hanging sticky yellow traps – just like the old-fashioned flypapers – among the plants. Brush the leaves repeatedly and this disturbs the adult whitefly which promptly flies to the yellow trap and meets a sticky end.

Another alternative is to release into the greenhouse a small parasitic wasp of whitefly called *Encarsia formosa*. This only works when temperatures are warm but when released into the house at the first sign of attack it will control whitefly and do harm to nothing else. If you use a living parasite of this kind it is not possible to use insecticide to control other pests because many of the insecticides will harm the wasp. You can get more information about the parasite and on sources of supply from The Royal Horticultural Society Gardens, Wisley, Nr. Woking, Surrey GU23 6QB.

◇

*I don't have much luck with cucumbers in the greenhouse. The
young plants often rot off at the bottom and even if they reach
maturity they're covered in mildew. The fruit is frequently mis-
shapen and bitter and much of it shrivels up when quite small.*

BILL   The growing of good cucumbers is often a problem that
many gardeners, amateur and indeed professional, find difficult to
solve. The commercial grower often grows them by the straw bale
method and he always has control of the temperature and humidity.
It is difficult if not impossible to grow good greenhouse cucumbers
in a greenhouse that is not artificially heated.

The ridge outdoor cucumbers are easy enough to grow providing
they are on a ridge of very rich soil and are not planted out until early
June. But greenhouse varieties of cucumbers are very different. The
straight varieties which produce female and male flowers on the
same plant must have the male flowers removed as soon as seen or
the female flowers may be fertilised and a bitter, Indian-club-
shaped fruit produced.

The greenhouse cucumber has the peculiar ability to produce
fruit without fertilisation. In most plants the flowers must be fertilised (or pollinated) in some fashion before a fruit can develop.

To make things easy for us, there are now all-female varieties of
greenhouse cucumber available such as 'Petita', 'Landora' or 'Fem-
spot', which are F_1 hybrids.

All greenhouse varieties should be grown on a mound of very rich
soil that has been warmed up before planting. As the white roots
come to the surface for air, moisture and nutrients, another inch or
so of rich compost is put on top of them and so growth proceeds.

Growing cucumbers on compost

Fruit is never allowed to form on the main stem, only on the laterals, and each lateral is stopped at one leaf past a fruit. High humidity and high temperatures are needed which can lead to mildew, so the use of a safe fungicidal spray is indicated at the first sign of disease.

Basal stem rot can be treated if the attack is slight. Dust sulphur or benomyl powder over the brown area and apply moist peat around the stem to encourage the formation of new roots. If the plant is severely affected, however, it will die. The cause is usually overwatering.

I would love to grow melons in my 6 ft × 8 ft (180 cm x 240 cm) greenhouse. I have an electric greenhouse fan-heater. Advice on cultivation and suitable varieties, please.

GEOFFREY Worth the effort just so you can savour sun-ripe warm melon! Sow the seeds two at a time into a peat or similar bio-degradeable container. Pull one out if both grow. A temperature around 65°F (18°C) will encourage quicker germination. Suitable varieties are 'Ogen' and 'Sweetheart,' with 'Gaylia F_1' a promising newcomer (I met 'Gaylia' only last summer). Sowing late March is early enough for frame or greenhouse cropping.

Melons require a humus-rich soil, so make up raised beds with compost or manure – put a hotbed of horse manure underneath and you can almost see them growing.

Alternatively, melons can be grown successfully in either pots or growing bags, though more attention must be given to watering. Water regularly, and pinch out the growing tip at the fourth leaf. Side-shoots will break and when these have three or four leaves stop again.

Alternatively, with 'Ogen' and 'Gaylia', first stop at two leaves, then train the side-shoots which grow up wires or netting. Stop when each has grown seven or eight leaves. Once fruit has set, stop any further lateral growth at two leaves past the fruitlet. Keep the atmosphere humid or the leaves will crisp. Do remember to polli-nate the female flowers. Pick a male bloom that is fully open and use it to pollinate the fully receptive female which can be identified by the swollen stem underneath the petals (males have straight flower stalks) – see illustration on page 64.

I overwinter my fuchsias in my cold greenhouse. Last March, when I came to repot them, I found all the roots had disappeared and the compost was full of small, fat, white grubs. I have noticed similar grubs in my window boxes and in the soil around my polyanthus plants.

DAPHNE   You have my sympathy, as two years ago I lost my entire fuchsia collection in just the same way. The grubs you describe are almost certainly the larvae of the vine weevil. The adult vine weevil feeds at night and is a particularly serious pest under glass, feeding on a wide range of plants. It is the grubs, however, which do most damage, destroying whole root systems if not detected soon enough. They are particularly fond of polyanthus – you are quite likely to find the grubs around the roots of plants beginning to look sick.

Adult vine weevils can be trapped in sacking or corrugated paper in the greenhouse – this can then be burnt. The grubs can be picked out of the compost or soil and squashed. Assuming any affected pot plants are worth saving, they should be repotted in fresh, clean compost, removing as much of the old, infested stuff as you can, and given a soil dressing of bromophos or HCH. Where vine weevils and their grubs have become really troublesome, it is as well to water the compost – or the soil if the problem was in the open ground – with HCH about once every three months to prevent reinfestation.

A vine weevil grub ($\frac{3}{4}$-1 inch long)

I have a greenhouse in which I grow mainly tomatoes and cucumbers. For two years the cucumbers have been plagued with red spider mites despite all attempts to destroy them. What can I do?

PETER   Greenhouse red spider mites are pale yellowish-brown really and only red in late summer as they start to hibernate. They thrive in hot, dry conditions and are serious pests of many greenhouse crops and house plants.

The first sign of attack is usually lack of leaf colour, a yellow speckling and general weakening of plant growth. Close inspection with a magnifying glass of the undersides of the leaves, especially the younger shoots up in the tips of the plant, will show the adults which are no more than half a millimetre long and have four pairs of short legs.

They breed rapidly and heavy infestations will produce fine cobwebbing over the growing points and side-shoots in the axils of the leaves. Really bad attacks usually occur from late May to September.

Keeping the atmosphere very humid is one way of deterring them. Misting over cucumbers with water several times a day, wetting the undersides of the leaves especially, will help the cucumbers no end and drown the red spider!

Strong, healthy plants that are growing fast are less likely to be attacked, while crowded greenhouses and plants under stress are very susceptible to red spider mite. It is often necessary to resort to chemical control and several applications at seven-day intervals will be needed of sprays based on dimethoate, formothion or derris. The latter should be used if the crops are nearing the harvest stage because it is a short-persistence chemical. Always check the manufacturers' instructions carefully when selecting sprays, especially for tender plants like cucumbers.

There is a predator of greenhouse red spider mite called *Phytoseiulus persimilis* which eats adults and immature mites but this insect needs warm temperatures to breed. Full details on this are available from Bunting and Sons, The Nurseries, Great Horkesley, Colchester, Essex CO6 4AJ.

Thorough hygiene, burning severely infected plants and old plant debris where possible in the autumn, is a good way to kill off hibernating adults. Foliar feeding with a seaweed-based fertiliser appears to deter red spider mite.

One day last week I noticed that a tomato plant was wilting as though short of water. I knew this wasn't the case but couldn't see anything wrong. Next day another three plants were showing the same symptoms and now six out of 12 plants have gone the same way. What has happened?

GEOFFREY This is a condition known as 'sleepy wilt' and it is a result of the roots being invaded by a fungus which lives in the soil. The fungus gains entry via the root-hairs and blocks the water conducting system, effectively cutting off the supply of moisture to the leaves, which in consequence wilt. In the cool of evening they may briefly regain turgidity.

Though mulching the soil heavily with peat may help by encouraging stem rooting, the crop will be so sparse it is best to pull up and destroy any plant showing signs of wilt. The disease will persist, so do not grow tomatoes on the same site unless you change or sterilise the soil. You could, however, succeed by grafting chosen varieties onto a suitable wilt-resistant rootstock.

I prefer to grow all tomatoes either on ring culture, or in pots or growing bags, rather than direct planting into possibly fungus-infected soil.

My greenhouse tomatoes are developing black spots on the base of the fruit which eventually rots. What causes this?

PETER   We call this condition blossom end rot because at the base of each fruit, furthest from the stalk, a sunken brown spot develops. With time the brown turns black and the fruit is inedible.

The most common cause is lack of calcium but the reason is usually inadequate and erratic watering. Two much potash – contained in tomato fertilisers – and also excess magnesium and ammonium/nitrogen fertiliser also aggravates this condition.

Where plants are kept well watered and grown in either good potting compost or good garden soil which is not excessively acid, or in good well-known brands of growing bags, this problem should not occur. I come across severe attacks most frequently where the tomatoes, and occasionally sweet peppers, are grown in a home prepared soil mix to no accepted formula.

At the first signs of attack, spraying the plants at fortnightly intervals with a solution of calcium nitrate or calcium chloride at 2 gm per litre will effect a cure.

Tomatoes do take up a considerable amount of water when growing fast and producing several bunches of fruit. While it is fairly easy to keep plants in soil well supplied with water, pot and growing bag plants need more frequent attention.

During hot weather, watering morning and evening is often necessary. With growing bags it is advisable to tuck the hand right into the inside corners of the bag and pull out small lumps of peat between the fingers. If these pieces are dry, several waterings will be needed to re-wet the peat compost.

Other crops affected by lack of calcium include lettuce, where the tips of the leaves are scorched, celery and chicory, where the hearts go black – usually on black, acid, peaty soil – and apples, where brown spots under the skin of fruits is called 'bitter pit'.

I have recently been given two tomato plants which I intend to grow in a south-facing sunroom attached to my house. As I've never grown tomatoes before, I would like to know if it is true that all side-shoots have to be removed, and if so, why. It seems such a waste!

GEOFFREY Like so many general rules in gardening this one needs some qualification. The small leafy side-shoots which grow from the leaf joints of single-stem tomatoes need to be removed. I wait until the shoots are an inch (2.5 cm) long and then just pinch them out between finger and thumb. The difference between a leaf shoot and an embryo flower truss is obvious at an early stage. Even so, have a care you do not prune out a flower truss by mistake.

Bush varieties of tomatoes do not require side-shooting. Popular varieties of these include 'Red Alert', 'Sigmabush' and 'The Amateur'. 'Alicante', 'Herald' and 'Golden Sunrise' are typical single-stem tomatoes and with these you need to pinch out the leafy side-shoots which grow from the angle formed between leaf and stem.

Side-shooting improves crop weight, encourages earlier ripening, reduces the risk of fungus disease by reason of better air circulation, and makes for an easily managed plant in limited space.

Can you give me some advice on how to look after an unheated greenhouse in winter and what I can use it for during these months?

BILL   Many greenhouses are unheated because of cost, and are used in winter for storing the pram, the bike, the beach ball, until the following summer. How to use an unheated greenhouse horticulturally in winter is more complicated.

First let's consider the many and various bulbs that can be grown in it. Most bulbs when grown in pots or bowls should have a long, cold, dark rooting period when they are outdoors, before being brought into either the home or the greenhouse. So if you want to grow bowls or pots of spring flowers such as hyacinths, daffodils, tulips, purple crocus, snowdrops, aconites, muscari or scillas, for display in the greenhouse, plant them around mid-September. Then put the containers in a north-facing position, covered with sand or ashes (not peat), where they will be cold and dark until a good root system has been produced and a little top growth. It is important when these bulbs are outdoors to protect them from mice by covering them with small-mesh wire netting.

The containers are brought into the greenhouse in early December. Flowers will be produced much earlier than if that plant was being grown outdoors. If the bowl or pot is taken into the house and put in a position where there is good light and a little warmth, flowers will be produced earlier still.

In the cold greenhouse other subjects can be grown quite satisfactorily and they include camellias in containers or large pots, pot azaleas and hydrangeas. Sweet peas can be sown in October along with schizanthus to overwinter in the cold greenhouse and these will flower all the earlier the following spring. Many annuals can be sown in September and would also flower early; they include godetia, larkspur, petunia, penstemon, nigella, nemophila, nicotiana, myosotis, calendula and lavatera. Perennial or biennial subjects like polyanthus or primrose could be sown a little earlier, and they would run into flower because of the protection.

If there is staging in the greenhouse, one or two rhubarb roots could be put underneath and be enclosed so that they are in the dark, to produce some forced rhubarb.

HOUSE PLANTS

EVERYBODY HAS AT ONE STAGE OR ANOTHER OWNED a house plant. So most of us know what it feels like to watch something wither away before our very eyes, despite our constant attempts to save it.

If you watch *Gardeners' Direct Line*, you may have noticed the way Peter usually knocks a house plant out of its pot before diagnosing what's wrong. The first time I saw him do it, I thought he was intent on doing away with the hapless thing altogether. Grasping it by the stem, he delivered a sharp tap to the edge of the pot and hey presto – there it was without its trousers on, so to speak.

'You can't find out what's wrong without looking down below,' he barked. The plant seemed to quake. Having checked the root system and the moisture level in the compost, Peter went on to sort out the problem. The plant was finally put back in its pot and we moved on.

The entire episode taught me one thing. Not that it is a good idea to have a look inside the pot when trying to cure house plants (although it clearly is), but that whatever one does with them should be done with *confidence*! Somehow or other the plant seems to pick this up and its own morale is generally given a boost. So long as your general demeanour is positive, the plant will be OK.

Convinced? No, neither am I. Time for the experts to take over.

JOHN THIRLWELL

All the leaves on my yucca have turned yellow and now the cane is starting to go soft. What have I done wrong, and is there any way of saving it?

PETER   Yucca leaves will stay green and quite healthy looking on the goodness in the thick woody stem for some weeks, even months. The appearance of yellow leaves usually indicates either a problem of long standing or a check to growth some time ago.

The stems are pretty tough and not prone to disease, so the appearance of soft rot on the woody trunk also indicates a fairly long-term malady. Most commonly the cause is too much water, especially in the winter when our days are short, the sunlight is weak and the nights cold.

Many of the tropical evergreen plants we use extensively as pot plants indoors grow in their native habitat at an even temperature of 70°F (20°C) or higher and in good strong daylight. All we can hope to do in average home temperatures, where the central heating goes off at night, is to keep the plant ticking over – a virtual hibernation – through the winter. This means going very carefully with the water and keeping the compost for tropical evergreens, including yucca, on the dry side. You are unlikely to harm them by giving too little water from November to February.

Once the leaves have yellowed and the stem has started to rot, it is quite a long job to get such plants growing strongly again. Put them in a light, warm place. Water sparingly and new root will usually be made. Don't be afraid carefully to knock the plant out of its pot now and again to check that the compost is not too wet and that the root tips are starting to grow. Once the roots do start to grow then the watering can be increased, especially in summer, and feeding started again.

Where the soft rot has almost girdled the stem, it may be necessary to take the green shoot off the stem and root it like a large cutting.

How do I take a cutting off my Swiss cheese plant as it is 7 feet tall and will soon be too big for the room?

GEOFFREY Cuttings of the Swiss cheese plant (*Monstera deliciosa*) are difficult to root because the large leaves lose so much moisture. The shoot is killed by drought before the new roots form.

Air layering is possibly the simplest method of propagation. Make an upward sloping cut in the stem 9 to 10 inches (23 to 25 cm) down from the tip and an inch (2.5 cm) long. Do not cut deeper than necessary, just enough to form a tongue. I use a few grains of sand or a sliver of matchstick to hold the cut open. Another way is to take a ring of bark a half-inch (1.25 cm) wide all round the stem. Dust whichever cut is made with rooting powder, pack the treated surface round with sphagnum moss, then wrap the whole lot in a sheet of plastic. I use electrician's tape to secure the package and make everything watertight. In a few weeks roots grow into the moss. Using a sharp pair of secateurs or a knife, clean-cut the stem just below the root-ball and pot the plantlet, moss as well, in a peat-based compost. *Do not over-firm* or the roots will get broken.

There is an alternative method; the top of a stem taken with two leaves will root. Dip the cut end in rooting powder before potting it up into a compost of 2 parts sand to 1 part peat. To cut down water loss, place the cutting complete with pot inside a clear plastic bag. Two hoops made from wire coat-hangers will hold the bag sides clear of the cutting leaves.

Stand the pot in a warm, light place – the bathroom windowsill is perfect.

I have an aspidistra and the leaves are turning brown at the ends. What is the reason for this?

DAPHNE   I feel slightly sorry for the aspidistra. Although its common name of cast iron plant describes its ability to withstand a certain amount of neglect, it isn't indestructable. Its popularity as an Edwardian houseplant was largely due to the fact that the kind of conditions it would tolerate were those it was likely to meet – chilly, draughty and poorly lit. Because the average temperature of the room was on the cold side, it didn't require much water either, hence its reputation for thriving on neglect.

The modern environment that the aspidistra has to face is usually vastly different. Just when it would like to settle down for a winter rest in a cool, light position, up goes the central heating and down goes the humidity. If the aspidistra gets the temperature it prefers during winter, it requires very little attention other than an occasional watering to ensure the compost doesn't remain bone-dry for weeks on end. Over-water it and the roots will rot and the leaves turn yellow and blotched, and if the plant is not rescued it will die. But in the centrally heated living-room it will continue to grow throughout the winter, and so the compost must be kept damp. If it is too dry, the leaf-tips will die – this, I think, is what is happening to yours. This also applies to the plant in summer – underwatering will produce these symptoms. In winter the plant can happily stand full sunlight, but in summer it must be kept out of the direct rays of the sun; scorch will also cause browning, but usually in patches on the leaves rather than at the ends. Sponging the leaves occasionally with water will help to keep them in good condition and helps to control red spider mite.

Don't repot your aspidistra until the pot is nearly bursting at the seams – the roots don't like being disturbed. A house plant fertiliser can be added to the water from time to time in summer, but don't overfeed. It is not unusual for a mature plant to produce flowers at ground level.

If your room is very warm, you may have more success with the variegated aspidistra, *Aspidistra elatior* 'Variegata', which is much more attractive but less hardy and therefore more suitable for modern home conditions.

I have a bottle garden but I can't keep it happy. The plants seem to die off in no time. Where am I going wrong, and can you recommend some foolproof plants for this situation?

DAPHNE   Overwatering is the main cause of bottle garden disaster. A bottle garden, properly planted and with compost of the right dampness, should be self-maintaining for many months, apart from having to remove dead and dying leaves when they occur to prevent setting up rots. If the compost looks sodden, or the glass steams up immediately the bung is replaced, then the bottle garden is too wet and the bung must be removed again to allow it to dry out or problems will soon arise.

Try to choose a clear glass bottle – tinted glass cuts down too much light. Use only sterile, peat-based compost – on no account use garden soil or old compost which will contain all sorts of pests and diseases. The depth of compost will depend on the size of bottle; a large carboy will take up to 6 inches (15 cm) but a small, modern, purpose-made bottle may only accommodate 2 to 3 inches (5 to 8 cm). This should be placed on top of 1 to 2 inches (2.5 to 5 cm) of pea gravel covered with a thin layer of charcoal – this assists drainage and keeps the compost sweet. It's easier if the compost is poured dry into the bottle and carefully watered afterwards by trickling water down the side, which also helps to clean the glass. It should be firmed lightly; if the bottle neck is too narrow to get your hand inside, a tool can be made for this by screwing a rubber doorstop onto the end of a cane.

Don't overplant – remember the plants in a healthy bottle garden will continue to grow. Unfortunately there are no totally reliable ones but, once established, plants in a bottle garden should theoretically be easy to keep in good condition. Plants to avoid are: those with flowers (dead flowers are hard to remove and will rot if they aren't); woolly-leaved ones as the air is too humid; and very rampant ones which will soon outgrow the bottle. Try maranta (prayer plant), pilea (aluminium plant), peperomia, small ferns, *Codiaeum variegatum* (croton), fittonia (snakeskin plant), *Ficus pumila* (weeping fig) and selaginella. Again, if the bottle neck is narrow, tape a teaspoon and table fork to the end of canes for planting and tidying up the top of the compost.

Always keep your bottle garden in good light. It will stand a south, west or east window during the winter, but move it just out of direct sunlight in summer – a north-facing window is ideal – or you'll cook the plants!

I have a bird of paradise plant which is 14 years old. It grows well with plenty of leaves but no flowers. What can I do about it?

GEOFFREY *Strelitzia reginae* is well named 'bird of paradise'. These plants take many years to reach the stage at which they produce flowers, and even then they will not flower under poor light conditions as I have discovered, but given 4 to 6 hours of sunlight a day they present no difficulty.

During the resting season, November to March, keep them in cool, frost-free conditions; a temperature of 50°F (10°C) is about the mark. They need just enough water to prevent the compost drying out completely.

Increase the water supply as growth quickens in spring and feed every two weeks during the growing period with high potash house-plant fertiliser. You will then, I think, be rewarded with flowers, provided the plant is mature enough, which it should be.

I have managed to keep a poinsettia plant from last Christmas. It has grown into a very large healthy plant and I am wondering what to do to make the bracts turn red.

PETER   The bracts of poinsettia, formed along with the tiny bead-like flowers, colour as the length of day shortens in the autumn. All green-leaved poinsettias that are growing healthily will colour if kept in natural daylight from early September onwards.

Where these plants are exposed to electric light, even for short periods in the autumn, they will think it is still summer, keep growing and remain green. House plants should therefore be kept in a spare room, where the light will not be switched on, until the colour starts to form. Once the colour has started it will keep forming and you need worry no more about artificial light.

Should you have no room without artificial light then the plant needs to be covered with a black polythene bag at sunset and uncovered at daybreak. We often see huge plants in homes and offices where they have been exposed to day and electric light. The best treatment here is to cut them back in August, dust the cut ends with some powdered charcoal to stop the flow of white milky sap (one or two burnt matches will supply sufficient charcoal for the average house plant). They will then grow again to 12 to 18 inches (30 to 45 cm) before producing red bracts in late December and January.

I have found the best way to treat Christmas gift-sized poinsettias is to stop watering in May. Leave the leafless stems in the dry compost in the pot out of sight through the summer, cut them back to 4 inches (10 cm) or so in August, water to get them growing and then feed regularly to produce colourful compact plants again.

How do you look after a cyclamen to ensure it lives as long as some of those you hear about?

BILL   I have seen some rare cyclamen and remember one particularly in the window of a terraced house with a corm the size of a saucer.

This plant, a pink variety with green foliage, was in full flower in January, surrounded by many other plants like the money plant, sleeping beauty, string of beads and a dozen others. This old lady, whose fingers were as green as grass, told me how she had nursed this cyclamen through 20 odd years. When it had finished flowering she kept feeding it with liquid blood every fortnight until late May. The plant was then taken out into the backyard (she had no garden), and the pot laid on its side in a sunny position. This was to give the plant a deserved rest until late August. The corm was then shaken out and repotted in a slightly larger pot in a mysterious mixture of loamy soil, dried cow manure, a little mortar rubble and soot. (She did say that in the last few years increasing infirmity, reduced amounts of mortar rubble and scarcity of cows and soot had made her use a modern loam-based compost.)

The plant, then virtually leafless, was taken indoors into a warm, dark position and kept just moist. As soon as new growths had appeared and were about half an inch high, the pot was brought out into full light. The pot was enclosed in an attractive china container with the space between the two containers filled with some moist peat and the fronds of selaginella (resurrection plant). This last subject can be as dry as snuff and when put in water or moist peat soon produces very attractive dark green fronds.

The green-fingered doyenne made one more point – that she never ever feeds the cyclamen when it is in bud or flower. Before and after yes, never during. So now you know!

All the leaves are dropping off my rubber plant. What can I do to stop this, and will the plant ever 'fill out' again?

DAPHNE   The rubber plant (*Ficus elastica* 'Decora' or *F. e.* 'Robusta') is not an easy plant to keep happy in the home, and it's a pity that so many people choose it as their first house plant – lack of success often discourages them for years. A much easier relative is *F. benjamina*, the weeping fig.

The rubber plant likes a warmish, light spot. Too little light and sudden changes of temperature are the usual causes of leaf drop, but so are overwatering and draughts. Repotting, especially when unnecessary, can also make a rubber plant shed its leaves.

Remove your rubber plant from its pot and check the roots. If they're soaking wet, it won't need any more water until the compost has dried out. If they smell appalling, they are obviously rotting and the plant is probably beyond remedial treatment. If watering doesn't appear to be the problem, check the position the plant is in. It should be in or near a draught-free window in winter to obtain maximum light, and just slightly back from this spot in summer so it isn't scorched by too much sunshine. The temperature should not drop below 55°F (13°C) and the plant should always be brought into the room in winter before the curtains are drawn. Halls and windowsills where the windows are regularly opened are unsuitable in winter because of draughts and sudden heat loss, and rooms where there are wide fluctuations of temperature should be avoided.

As rubber plants get older and more tree-like, it is natural for the oldest leaves to drop off.

Providing your rubber plant is alive, the best treatment to correct legginess is to air-layer it. This consists of wounding the bark around the leaf-joint below the last healthy leaf, dusting on a little hormone rooting powder and then surrounding the wound with damp peat, soil-less cutting compost or sphagnum moss. This is covered with polythene, tied top and bottom. After about two months roots will have been made into the peat. The stem can be cut below these and the top half potted up in potting compost to make a new plant. Usually the remainder of the plant will produce side branches, but take care with the watering until new leaves appear – it won't need much.

Air-layering a rubber plant

I have just been given a wax plant as a present and want to look after it properly.

BILL   The marvellous *Hoya* family consists of some 200 species, and their name is in honour of Thomas Hoy, one-time gardener to the Duke of Northumberland at Sion House.

The two species most commonly grown here are the twining *Hoya carnosa*, the true wax plant, and the decumbent evergreen *H. bella*, usually known as the miniature wax plant. Both are very beautiful subjects when in flower, and indeed out of flower, especially *carnosa* which has attractive deep green leaves. The leaves of *H. bella* are much smaller and slightly greyish-green. Both varieties are probably natives of Malaysia and are fairly tender, with *H. bella* requiring a warmer position than *H. carnosa*. *H. bella*, because of its habit, is a perfect plant for the hanging basket, whereas *H. carnosa*, being a clamberer, needs some canes or wires to get hold of.

Both are intolerant of a dry position and, perhaps peculiarly, do not like direct sunlight. When grown in a dwelling house it is important to remember that atmospheric humidity must be increased, and this is best done by the double container method of having the pot in a larger container and filling the space between the two with fine peat or florist's moss, which is kept just moist. Pests are not usually a problem, except for the scale insect. For the person with the odd plant, carefully picking these off as they appear is better than constant spraying with an insecticide, which anyway runs off scale insects like water off a duck's back.

One peculiarity about this family is that it is very important not to pinch off the dead flowers because it is from their base that next year's flowers will be produced.

Regular fortnightly feeding from March to November, with a high potash liquid fertiliser, is necessary. Little water and lower humidity in winter are musts.

A miniature wax plant grown in a hanging basket

I am quite successful in taking cuttings from African violets.
They grow very well, but I can't get them to bloom.

BILL   No house plant has increased more in popularity this last
20 years than the saintpaulia, commonly called the African violet.
Today there are many marvellous varieties that can be raised from
seed, such as 'Velvet Gem', 'Grandiflora Pink', 'Grandiflora Violet
Blue' and 'Velvet Cascade'. This is a subject that likes to have good
light, otherwise it will not flower, and be warm but not too hot. It
certainly needs a non-arid atmosphere, which is why often the best
saintpaulias in the dwelling house are in either the bathroom or the
kitchen. The modern variety 'Velvet Cascade' is particularly suitable for hanging baskets because of its habit, and propagation of this
variety is similar to the ordinary erect-growing varieties, by seeds or
leaf cuttings.

Seeds should be sown in March, but leaf cuttings are taken any
time between April and the end of September. The fully developed,
but not old, leaf should be taken with about an inch of stalk and be
inserted in coarse sand, burying only a small part of the blade. The
sand is kept just moist but never ever wet, and the position should be
in full light but not direct sunlight. Ideally the container of leaf
cuttings should be enclosed in a clear-film polythene bag until new
growth indicates that satisfactory rooting has taken place, when the
bag is removed. The plantlets are potted up separately in 3-inch
(8-cm) pots in a peat-based compost.

Obviously like produces like, so you take leaf cuttings from known
floriferous plants. This maxim applies throughout the gardening
world, whether you are propagating saintpaulias, lilacs, pansies,
tomatoes or whatever. Just as a milkfloat horse has no chance of
producing a Derby winner, neither will a non-flowering African
violet produce a free-flowering youngster.

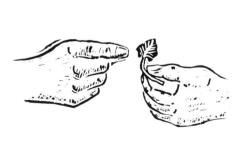

Rooting cuttings from an African violet

*Can you give me advice on how to treat my amaryllis? The
flowers have died but there are still plenty of leaves.*

DAPHNE   An amaryllis (*Hippeastrum vittatum hybridum*) is quite easy
to keep from year to year, but if it flowered around Christmas, it was
because the bulb had been specially prepared for early flowering.
Normal flowering time is spring, but it sometimes takes a prepared
bulb a year or two to settle down again into its true flowering
routine.

The dry bulb should have been planted in a 6 inch (15 cm) pot or
half-pot in a soil-less compost. There is no need for it to be repotted
annually – pot-bound bulbs flower better. Re-potting should only
take place every 3 to 5 years, when offsets can be removed if required
to make new plants.

Remove the dead flowers if you do not want to save the seed, and
continue watering until the autumn. The pot can be placed outside
in a sunny spot if wished. Feed with a houseplant fertiliser according
to the manufacturer's instructions throughout the summer. In early
autumn, stop watering and the leaves will eventually die off. Keep
the bulb, in its compost and pot, in a cool but dry and frost-free place
to 'rest'. In early spring, bring into a warm, light position, and new
growth will appear, when watering should start again.

New plants can sometimes be obtained by sowing the ripe seed in
a good peat-based seed compost. The young plants should be kept in
active growth for the first few years while the bulb is developing. It
will take at least five years to obtain a flowering-sized bulb by this
method.

*All the leaves are dropping off my indoor azalea and the buds
have stopped opening. I am feeding it well so I don't know what
has gone wrong.*

DAPHNE   The Indian azalea (*Rhododendron simsii, Azalea indica*) is
almost hardy in Great Britain, and the symptoms you describe are
almost certainly those caused by the plant being placed under stress
by moving it from the cool, humid conditions it enjoys in the nursery
to the hot, dry atmosphere of the living-room. The buds fail to open
and gradually all the leaves are shed until the plant is a sorry sight.
Feeding will only make matters worse – a sick plant should never be
fed and Indian azaleas require careful feeding, like all members of
the *Rhododendron* family. They are, however, lime-haters and if

watered with ordinary tap water that is hard, the leaves will eventually turn yellow as the plant becomes starved of iron. This can be avoided by either watering with soft water or using a weak solution of a soluble rhododendron fertiliser containing iron, magnesium and manganese in a 'chelated' form which will not be 'locked up' and therefore made unavailable to the plant by the calcium in the water.

The 'indoor' azalea is one of the few house plants whose compost must be kept *wet*, not just damp, at all times, otherwise the problems you describe will occur. It really isn't happy as a house plant; the only places it will thrive in are light rooms where the temperature does not exceed 60°F (16°C), and cool conservatories. Where warmer conditions are unavoidable, the compost should be misted at least once a day, and the pot placed in a larger outer container of wet peat, sand, pea-gravel or perlite to increase humidity.

After flowering and when the danger of frost has passed, the plant can be placed outdoors in a shady spot, making sure it never becomes dry at the roots. Repotting will only be necessary when the plant becomes potbound. Flower buds will form during the late summer – the best way of ensuring a good display from these is to bring the plant into a cool, frost-free place with plenty of light in autumn, and move it into a warmer room once the buds have finally opened.

I have several citrus plants grown from pips and I am wondering if they will ever bear fruit. Also, what causes the leaves to turn yellow?

DAPHNE   It's quite easy to grow orange, lemon and grapefruit plants from pips and they make interesting house plants. In theory they should eventually flower and fruit but they may have to grow quite large before this can happen and as they are seedlings it is difficult to predict whether the fruit will be palatable or even eatable, but providing you have the space and the patience it is an interesting experiment.

Citrus plants dislike hot, dry, stuffy conditions, especially in winter, and so a cool (about 45° to 50°F, 7° to 10° C), sunny position should be provided from September to May. During the summer the plants are happier if placed outside. They are often troubled with aphid and whitefly infestation, which can be treated using an insecticide recommended for house plants.

Yellowing of the leaves is usually caused by watering with hard, limy water, or not using an ericaceous compost for potting. If adequate soft water is not available, the problem can be overcome by watering once or twice a year with sequestered iron or a sequestrene-based plant 'tonic'.

If you want to grow citrus plants for fruit, it's best to buy a variety suitable for home cultivation. *Citrus mitis*, the calamondin orange, flowers and bears small, bitter fruit nearly all the year round. Under greenhouse conditions *Citrus sinensis*, the sweet orange, bears reasonably eatable fruit 2¹/₂ inches (6 cm) in diameter. The Seville orange, *Citrus aurantica*, whose fruits are used for marmalade, makes a prickly bush 3 feet (90 cm) high. *Citrus limon meyeri* and *Citrus limon* 'Ponderosa' are dwarf lemon trees with useable lemons, but they must be given the right conditions to produce fruit.

Is it better to germinate an avocado stone in water, or can it be put straight into compost like other seeds?

GEOFFREY Avocado stones, which are similar in shape and size to a pullet's egg, are not difficult to germinate.

To start the seed, for that after all is what the stone is, into growth, just sow it into moist compost. This is one of those seeds which germinate quicker at a high temperature, so pop the pot inside a polythene bag and stand it near a warm radiator or in the airing

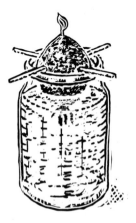

Germinating an avocado over water

cupboard. Once germinated, move the pot into a light but not too warm room.

You can stand the stone in a water-filled glass or in a jar with its base just immersed. The stone turns bright pink, then splits and grows a shoot. Once this happens, pot it up in the usual way.

How do I look after a date palm grown from a stone? It is now about 6 inches (15 cm) high.

DAPHNE Many successful date palms (*Phoenix dactylifera*) started life as stones pushed into the compost of other plants at Christmas. If this is the case, they should be removed as soon as possible as the palm grows quite quickly, often getting too large for the average home.

Date stones germinate best at a temperature of 70°F (20°C) to 75°F (24°C) and can take several months to appear. They will need repotting quite frequently until they reach the size when it becomes impracticable. I use a soil-based compost – John Innes No. 1 for small plants, No. 2 for potting on into pots over 4¹/₂ inches (11 cm) in diameter, and No. 3 for very big palms in large containers.

There are other date palms which make more suitable house plants, for example, *Phoenix roebelinii*, the pygmy date palm, and *P. canariensis*, the Canary date palm. These are usually available from larger house plant nurseries.

It is quite possible to grow a coconut palm (*Cocos nucifera*) from a coconut by half-submerging it in a shallow pot of John Innes No. 1 compost and keeping it at a temperature of 75°F (24°C). The true coconut palm makes an unsatisfactory house plant as it needs 'stove house' conditions, under which it has the potential to grow 100 feet (30 m) or more. The coconut palm that is usually sold as a house-plant is *cocos weddeliana (Syagrus weddeliana)* which also can be quite tricky to grow as it only thrives under the warm, humid conditions usually found in a heated conservatory.

POSTSCRIPT

WELL, IF YOU'VE GOT THIS FAR THEN YOU'RE clearly pretty determined to crack this gardening business. I congratulate you on your perseverance. It may be, of course, that you're one of those people who'd rather read about something than actually *do* it, but there's no more book left, so now you're going to have to get out there and actually do some gardening!

Before you go, a few words of advice from one who knows a thing or two about how to *avoid* gardening. First, if your neighbours make you feel your unkempt patch is letting the street down, tell people you're growing a wild garden – that's a fairly good one to use in these days of conservation. (Actually, as a conservationist myself I think gardens *should* be more 'wild'.) And, secondly, do a lot of sitting in your garden at week-ends. That will make them *think* you're keen, even if you're only sleeping off the excesses of last night at the 'Three Ferrets'.

Perhaps the most successful way of coping with a garden that is an eyesore is to buy thicker sitting-room curtains. But even *I* think that's cheating a little . . .

Anyway, whatever you do – do it slowly. Plants run to seasons and not to clocks, thank heavens. So take your time and enjoy it.

Happy gardening!

JOHN THIRLWELL

INDEX

Page numbers in *italic* refer to illustrations.